3 0738 00152 3553

DISCARD

BOOMER
VOLUNTEER
ENGAGEMENT
Facilitator's Tool Kit

Jill Friedman Fixler
and Beth Steinhorn

In partnership with VolunteerMatch

D1534562

AuthorHouse™
1663 Liberty Drive
Bloomington, IN 47403
www.authorhouse.com
Phone: 1-800-839-8640

© 2010 Jill Friedman Fixler and Beth Steinhorn. All rights reserved.
www.jffixler.com

No part of this book may be reproduced, stored in a retrieval system,
or transmitted by any means without the written permission of the author.

In partnership with VolunteerMatch
www.volunteermatch.org

Book design by Lisa McGuire
Communication & Design

First published by AuthorHouse 5/26/2010

Library of Congress Control Number: 2010906155

ISBN: 978-1-4520-1538-5 (e)
ISBN: 978-1-4520-1537-8 (sc)

Printed in the United States of America
Bloomington, Indiana

This book is printed on acid-free paper.

This Facilitator's Tool Kit is a companion to the book,

Boomer Volunteer Engagement:

Collaborate Today, Thrive Tomorrow.

Use these tools in conjunction with the book.

This Tool Kit is available in both print version
and as an eBook. You can order these resources at
www.BoomerVolunteerEngagement.org

CONTENTS

FOREWORD

Imagine a world in which your nonprofit organization has all the resources it needs to serve more clients, deliver more programs, strengthen its staff, spread its message more widely, and increase its financial stability. Envision a future in which nonprofits have a pool of talented, skilled, and passionate individuals on call to build organizational capacity by serving as consultants, strategists, marketing gurus, ambassadors, innovators, mentors, fund-raisers, and direct service teammates.

So began our book, *Boomer Volunteer Engagement: Collaborate Today, Thrive Tomorrow*, which has since helped nonprofits across North America build capacity through skilled and dedicated volunteers. Since its publication in 2008, we have heard from thousands of people who have used the book with their organizations. We have worked closely with our many clients as they used *Boomer Volunteer Engagement* as a guide to build organizational capacity through high-impact volunteer engagement. During this time, we were inspired to help our clients take this work to the next level – by partnering with volunteers to lead strategic volunteer engagement initiatives. As a result, we compiled this Tool Kit to share the resources needed for staff and volunteers to co-facilitate such an endeavor.

While the world, the economy, and the nonprofit sector have undergone many changes since the publication of *Boomer Volunteer Engagement*, the process laid out by the book continues to work. In fact, this capacity-building model is even more relevant in challenging times. *Boomer Volunteer Engagement* guides nonprofits through a process of organizational change – from a traditional culture of volunteer management, in which staff drives the work of volunteers, to a culture of volunteer engagement, in which volunteers and staff partner to achieve meaningful results for the organization. As times have changed, one thing has remained constant in our work with organizations: the key to surviving and thriving through changing conditions is to continuously access the resources needed to address emerging needs. Surviving and thriving through a difficult economy or through unexpected challenges such as epidemics or disasters is about being nimble and responsive. Being entrenched in old ways does not sustain organizations through changing times; the ability to innovate in response to emerging trends sustains organizations. The facility to quickly access human capital in the form of skills, talents, and networks helps them thrive.

Shifting to such a culture of volunteer engagement does not happen overnight, but, if approached with intention and strategic focus, it can happen relatively quickly. The book *Boomer Volunteer Engagement* advocates for initiating change in small, discrete ways through a pilot project that demonstrates the power of high-impact volunteer engagement. In our work with organizations throughout North America, pilot projects were the start of a larger, organization-wide shift because change begets change. When one small pilot project is well-planned and well-executed, and when the successes of that pilot are strategically shared, momentum builds.

We shared this work with the California state libraries. Over a two-year period, we worked with 37 libraries to pilot initiatives using volunteers to build their libraries' capacity to meet the growing needs of their communities. On the surface, the results are impressive: volunteers worked with library staff to develop new programs, deliver services to new audiences, improve their technologies, and create volunteer leaders who are self-directed and who build their own teams of new volunteers. On a deeper level, the impacts are nothing short of extraordinary. Their work has successfully repositioned the library as a community asset in tough economic times. As the State of California faces unprecedented budget crises, libraries that participated in these pilot programs not only have proven models for successfully utilizing broad generations of volunteers, they also have cultivated a powerful corps of volunteers who are now passionate advocates in the community, fighting for their library's future. By welcoming innovation, they increased event and program participation, significantly deepened community partnerships, and are called upon as resources and experts by their municipalities and neighboring organizations. In short, by focusing their volunteers' efforts in high-impact, strategic ways, they are now key players in the landscape of their communities.

Shifting from a traditional practice of volunteer management to an innovative culture of volunteer engagement has far-reaching benefits. Your organization will gain access to the abundant skills of multiple generations of volunteers. By strategically accessing this human capital, your team will be more nimble and better positioned to respond to any future circumstance. Your staff will have the capacity to do work that is critical and plays to their strengths, while volunteers partner to achieve other mission-based work. As an added bonus: your staff and your volunteers will enjoy their work more because they will have teammates with complementary talents, partners and allies to meet the challenges, and friends and colleagues with whom to celebrate the successes.

The book *Boomer Volunteer Engagement* details all of these reasons, plus more, for intentionally shifting from volunteer management to volunteer engagement. In this Tool Kit, we present additional tools designed to help your team pilot this change using volunteers as co-leaders of the initiative. In a volunteer engagement culture, authenticity is key. When an organization decides to implement an initiative to demonstrate the powerful potential of collaborative volunteer engagement, having a staff person and a volunteer co-lead the initiative is an important way to demonstrate that the effort is sincere. Furthermore, having a skilled volunteer partner with staff as a co-facilitator helps to share the workload and adds skills to the process. In the following modules, you will find all the tools your organization needs to cultivate volunteer and staff co-facilitators plus the tools they will need to successfully facilitate a Boomer Volunteer Engagement Initiative. By modeling the collaboration from the very start, your initiative will be poised for success. At the end of this eight-month endeavor, your organization will be stronger for tomorrow, your community will be better served today, and your staff and volunteers will find the journey along the way much more enjoyable and rewarding.

—Jill Friedman Fixler and
Beth Steinhorn

ACKNOWLEDGMENTS

Many people have contributed directly and indirectly to the development of this Tool Kit. The work is built on the foundation laid by the book *Boomer Volunteer Engagement: Collaborate Today, Thrive Tomorrow*, co-authored by Jill Friedman Fixler and Sandie Eichberg, with Gail Lorenz, CVA. While *Boomer Volunteer Engagement* was inspired by a vision of what could be in a world that truly harnessed the power and potential of the Baby Boomer generation, this collection of tools and resources is a direct result of what has actually been done by our clients, partners, colleagues, volunteers, and funders.

We are thankful to all our clients who continue to inspire us to develop, apply, and refine the volunteer engagement tools that form the core of both the book and this Tool Kit. We extend a heartfelt thanks to our partner in piloting the volunteer center model for this Tool Kit, Metro Volunteers. We are grateful to Kristy Judd, Executive Director of Metro Volunteers, for joining this endeavor and to Gary Renville for his early support of this project. To the Operations Team at Metro Volunteers – Steve Norris, Sandie Eichberg, Hannah Levy, and Kristy Judd – thank you for accepting the leadership of this new initiative and managing it with such commitment, professionalism, patience, and passion. While the Operations Team shepherded the process, it was the Facilitators who brought the program out into the field and worked directly with community nonprofits. To Karen Blackman, Margaret Browne, Sandie Eichberg, Hannah Levy, Pam Mayhew, and Patty Rousch – all Baby Boomers yourselves – thank you for your pioneering spirit and passionate belief that volunteerism truly improves the effectiveness of nonprofits.

To the other brave pioneers in this project, the nonprofit organizations who stepped up to take on this initiative, we also are grateful. To the Autism Society of Colorado (www.autismcolorado.org), the Butterfly Pavilion (www.butterflies.org), Metro Volunteers (www.metrovolunteers.org), Operation Frontline (www.strength.org/operation_frontline), Providers Resource Clearinghouse (www.prccolorado.org), and Stepping Stones (www.stepping-stonesfamily.com), thank you for your ability to envision a bigger future for your organizations and your trust in the skills of volunteers to get you there.

This Tool Kit would not have been possible without the support and shared vision of our funders. Rose Community Foundation provided the innovation grant to support this work, which was matched by funds from VolunteerMatch. Therese Ellery at Rose Community Foundation has been a supportive and enthusiastic colleague and our collaborations with Sarah Christian, Director of Strategic Partnerships at VolunteerMatch, continue to be among our most rewarding and enjoyable partnerships. We also are grateful to the Jay and Rose Phillips Family Foundation for their support of the Metro Volunteers pilot.

Our acknowledgments would not be complete without thanking Linda Puckett, Director of Client Relations at JFFixler Group, and Jennifer Rackow, JFFixler Group Senior Strategist. Both of them continuously add new perspective to our work, share their expertise, challenge us to think big, and always go above and beyond. And, we thank other valued colleagues whom we consider part of the JFFixler family. Kim Leisner Kramer was a fabulous copy editor. Lisa McGuire, our talented designer, once again brought our concept to life in a beautiful and user-friendly medium.

Finally, we thank the many nonprofit workers (both staff and volunteers) who inspired us to take our work to the next step and create this Tool Kit. Their commitment to volunteer engagement continues to motivate us to develop new tools and strategies to help them achieve their goals, dreams, and missions, and ultimately make the world a better place.

Introduction

The book *Boomer Volunteer Engagement: Collaborate Today, Thrive Tomorrow* lays out the foundation for organizational change towards a culture of truly collaborative volunteer engagement, harnessing the powerful resource of Boomer volunteers. Since the publication of the book, we have gathered information and stories from those who have used the book to guide their own organizations and seen meaningful outcomes. Through those stories and our continued consulting work across North America, we know that the model brings about important results, from small, local organizations to multi-level, national organizations. The Boomer volunteer engagement model is a powerful capacity-building tool and the impacts are far-reaching – with volunteer teams launching new programs to reach more clients, bringing new professional skills to the organization to enhance marketing, technology, and human resource practices, increasing fund development, and much, much more.

This Tool Kit is designed to make it as easy as possible for your nonprofit to successfully – and sustainably – engage Boomer volunteers and the generations that follow in impactful, meaningful roles that substantively help your organization. Each tool was developed through our work in the field and inspired by reports from those who have already used the book *Boomer Volunteer Engagement* with their organizations. This process is designed to model the collaborative nature of volunteer engagement from the very start by engaging volunteers as leaders, partnering with staff to achieve this change. In other words, this Tool Kit takes the process of volunteer engagement to new heights by engaging volunteers as co-facilitators of the process. By demonstrating the potential of having Boomer volunteers empowered to lead this initiative, your organization will be able to more quickly embrace the change you wish to see.

We created the Tool Kit for all organizational leaders who can imagine a bigger future for their organizations. CEOs, Board Members, Directors of Volunteer Services, Auxiliary Presidents, Operations Directors, and others can use these tools to engage staff and volunteer co-facilitators to lead a volunteer engagement initiative. No matter what your position, one of the most important contributions you can make to the process is to be thoughtful and strategic about the people you cultivate to fill the roles of co-facilitators and Task Force Members. Selecting the right people for these positions will go a long way to leverage the process for success.

This Tool Kit contains the resources that you and your organization need to swiftly and systematically engage co-facilitators and members of a Boomer Volunteer Engagement Task Force to implement a volunteer engagement initiative. The Kit contains everything you and they will need to:

- Gain support and commitment from organizational leaders to embrace Boomer volunteer engagement as an essential, integral, and valuable business strategy.
- Cultivate and engage two volunteer engagement co-facilitators (one staff member and one volunteer) who will shepherd the organization through the step-by-step process.
- Train those co-facilitators to oversee a volunteer engagement Task Force, comprised of both staff and volunteers.
- Facilitate the Task Force's operations through a detailed timeline, meeting agendas, discussion guides, and more.
- Under the leadership of the Task Force, identify, select, and implement a pilot project that both addresses a strategic need of the organization and demonstrates the power of high-impact volunteer engagement.
- Assess the impacts of the pilot project.
- Identify next steps that will enable your organization to leverage the successes of the pilot project and sustain a culture of volunteer engagement.

The Tools – Why?

The original book focuses specifically on engaging Boomers as volunteers, yet we know that the strategies are effective for generations beyond Boomers and can be applied to successfully engage all generations of skilled volunteers for high-impact, meaningful work. Additionally, we sought to take volunteer engagement to another level, utilizing volunteers to lead the initiative. We asked ourselves and our community partners, "Now that we've proven that volunteers are such an untapped resource of experience and skill, how can Boomers and the generations that follow help lead organizations in their efforts to more effectively engage other skilled volunteers and build organizational capacity?" We explored how volunteers could help organizations develop and implement innovative volunteer engagement practices to help their organizations thrive. Could they serve as facilitators of the process, holding the team accountable? Could they partner with staff members who may be overwhelmed by the prospects of adding another new initiative to their plates? Could they oversee and manage such an initiative? And, through this approach, how could staff and volunteer leaders reinvent the way they get work done in order to build their own capacity and, ultimately, fulfill the organization's mission more fully?

We knew that the answer to all of these questions could be a resounding, "Yes!" We wanted to test and refine the tools. Through a valued partnership with Metro Volunteers, a volunteer center in Denver, Colorado (www.MetroVolunteers.org), we developed all the tools needed for a nonprofit to model the volunteer engagement process by engaging trained volunteers to serve as facilitators of this process. Working with Metro Volunteers, we recruited and trained six experienced Boomers to serve as facilitators with local nonprofits. The facilitators brought skills and professional experience to their facilitator roles, and included volunteers who had worked as a corporate executive, municipal volunteer coordinator, nonprofit executive, government manager, and business professor. Each facilitator guided a task force from one nonprofit through the process of Boomer volunteer engagement, as laid out in the book. They convened meetings, facilitated Task Force discussions, coached on the exercises, held the team accountable, established benchmarks for progress, and facilitated the evaluation of results. In other words, nonprofits built their capacity by engaging a volunteer leader who took the initiative from conception through implementation (rather than being told what to do and how to do it), while being supported by staff (rather than being managed by staff). We know your organization can do the same. This Tool Kit contains all of the tools needed to engage a volunteer facilitator to partner with a staff member and guide your organization through a high-impact volunteer engagement initiative that will tangibly build your organizational capacity beyond what staff alone can accomplish.

As a companion to the book, *Boomer Volunteer Engagement*, this Tool Kit refers to the book frequently, and has clear and useful tactics on how to implement the volunteer engagement process with your organization. In *Boomer Volunteer Engagement*, we recommend establishing a Task Force that conducts a needs assessment, identifies a pilot project, develops volunteer positions, oversees a Work Plan, and measures progress of a pilot project in order to demonstrate the power and potential of high-impact volunteer engagement. The tools in this Kit will help you launch that process by defining the roles of staff and volunteer partners who will convene and facilitate that Task Force (co-facilitators), guiding the work of the Task Force, establishing goals and benchmarks, and holding the Task Force accountable for delivering and communicating results. The Tool Kit includes position descriptions and recruitment materials for co-facilitators and Task Force members, a comprehensive timeline for co-facilitators to use (complete with meeting agendas, discussion guides, and exercises), and assessment tools to help organizations apply the learning from the pilot toward their next capacity-building endeavor.

The Tool Kit is meant to guide you through the Boomer volunteer engagement process and is designed to take approximately eight months, including two months at the beginning to cultivate co-facilitators and give them time to prepare. The work of the Task Force will take approximately six months, and could take longer depending on the scope of your particular pilot project. The meeting agendas and discussion guides are tools for the co-facilitators to use as they facilitate the Task Force's work. The detailed meeting agendas specify a timeframe for completing most of the exercises in the book *Boomer Volunteer Engagement*. These are suggestions. We hope that you will adapt these agendas and timelines to your organization's and team's particular needs, style, and timeframe.

To summarize, this Tool Kit provides a process that wraps around the steps outlined in the book *Boomer Volunteer Engagement.* The relationship between the Tool Kit and the book looks like the graphic on the following page. While a graphic representation is a useful reference, stories of how the process actually worked with organizations are invaluable. The following selected case studies demonstrate how some of the participating pilot programs implemented a volunteer engagement initiative for sustainable results and they paint a vivid picture of what is possible when volunteers lead the effort. As these examples show, when nonprofits pilot change in small, measurable ways, change comes more easily in other areas and, in just a short time, organizations will have shifted to a culture of volunteer engagement.

PREPARATION

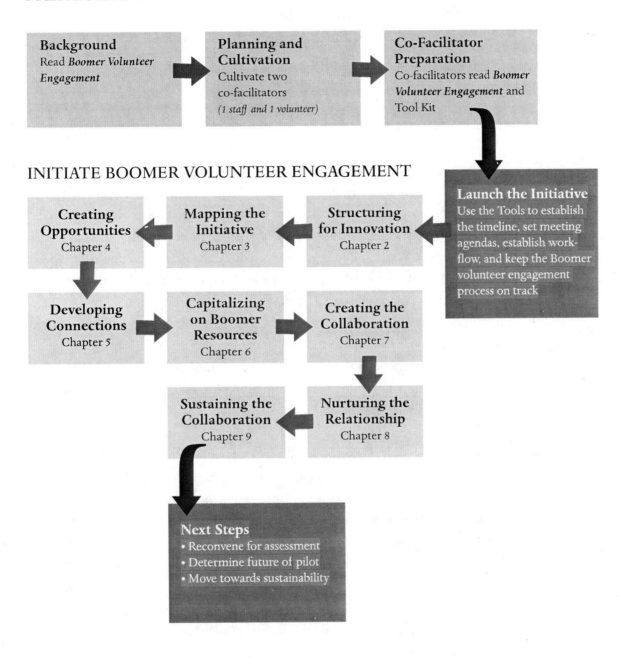

Background
Read *Boomer Volunteer Engagement*

Planning and Cultivation
Cultivate two co-facilitators
(1 staff and 1 volunteer)

Co-Facilitator Preparation
Co-facilitators read *Boomer Volunteer Engagement* and Tool Kit

INITIATE BOOMER VOLUNTEER ENGAGEMENT

Creating Opportunities
Chapter 4

Mapping the Initiative
Chapter 3

Structuring for Innovation
Chapter 2

Launch the Initiative
Use the Tools to establish the timeline, set meeting agendas, establish workflow, and keep the Boomer volunteer engagement process on track

Developing Connections
Chapter 5

Capitalizing on Boomer Resources
Chapter 6

Creating the Collaboration
Chapter 7

Sustaining the Collaboration
Chapter 9

Nurturing the Relationship
Chapter 8

Next Steps
• Reconvene for assessment
• Determine future of pilot
• Move towards sustainability

CASE STUDY

OPERATION FRONTLINE
Expanding Volunteer Roles to Increase Capacity
Beyond What Staff Alone Can Accomplish

These volunteer leaders are very highly skilled and they are able to act and think like staff members and represent Operation Frontline well. Because of each of their unique skills, they are a huge asset to us and to the class participants. —Victoria Pane, Volunteer Coordinator, Operation Frontline

Operation Frontline provides a strong educational foundation in nutrition, cooking, and household budgeting through specialized courses for adults, children, and teens. The organization provides knowledge and skills so that children facing hunger are surrounded by healthy foods where they live, learn, and play. Operation Frontline conducts educational courses for families with limited resources to educate children and adults on how to prepare healthy meals at home, using foods that are commonly available in stores and from emergency food providers. The goal of the courses is to promote making the healthiest food choices possible, even with limited resources. Adult and teen participants receive groceries at the end of each class to practice the recipes they have learned at home. The instructors are chefs and nutritionists who volunteer their time to teach lifelong cooking skills, practical nutrition information, and food budgeting strategies that participants can use right away and take into the future.

When Operation Frontline first engaged a volunteer facilitator to develop a volunteer engagement initiative, it had 10 people on staff and they were interviewing and training approximately 30 new volunteers each month. Their programs depended on volunteers – many of them highly skilled – to serve as chef instructors, nutrition instructors, financial planners, and support volunteers. But the number of classes offered depended entirely on the staff's ability to coordinate the scheduling, shopping, preparation, and set up of each program. In working with their facilitator, the members of the Operation Frontline Task Force identified that their greatest area of need was at this level of coordinating volunteers and course preparation. At that point, this coordinating level was reserved for paid staff alone. If they could only expand their staff's capacity to coordinate the schedules and class preparation, they could dramatically increase the number of program offerings – and thereby expand the clients served and their impact in the community.

The Task Force developed a Work Plan designed to achieve its vision, which was to create a volunteer program that relies on volunteers, no matter their skill-set, to consistently complete tasks previously done by staff members that do not require the staff's specific skill-set.

In other words, they envisioned a future in which volunteers could do what staff alone had been doing in order to more fully achieve their mission. The Work Plan detailed the eventual impacts and outcomes of such a vision. The initial impacts would be:

- Maximizing staff time and skills, allowing them to increase focus on courses and reach more families across the state.
- Creating new, more flexible volunteer positions that would leverage the many volunteers who were interested in serving, but who are not qualified to serve as chefs and nutritionists. Through these new positions, more volunteers would be engaged and leveraged for the skills and passions they do possess.

The sustained outcomes would be:

- To have enough trained and skilled volunteers to fulfill their strategic priorities in terms of program delivery – specifically, completing all of their courses, orientations, and office administrative tasks.
- To utilize volunteers of all ages, skills, and time constraints in multiple capacities so that more families would be served through Operation Frontline educational programs, helping them and the others in their communities live healthier lives with the resources they have available.
- To free staff to steward other initiatives, including responding to the increasing interest from other agencies in collaborating to bring Operation Frontline classes to those organizations' constituents, thereby helping them and their communities live healthier lives with the resources they have available.

As a result of this Work Plan, Operation Frontline engaged a pilot cohort of team leaders who coordinate their own teams of volunteer chefs, nutritionists, shoppers, and others. No longer is staff solely responsible for coordinating all these individuals and holding them accountable. More importantly, the number of courses conducted and families served are not limited to what staff can handle. As a result, five new classes were offered in the first trimester, reaching an estimated 60 new families, and saving staff 180 hours of work. All of the new team leader volunteers are continuing with the program and will coordinate another five to eight classes in this next trimester, while additional team leaders are being cultivated as well. The goal is to continue to replicate this model to grow Operation Frontline class offerings further.

CASE STUDY

BUTTERFLY PAVILION
Engaging a Task Force for Long-Term Change

The Task Force was a really productive group for us. We will use the Task Force in a leadership capacity in the future, as we have been seeking a group like this but hadn't been able to create one until now. —Kris Pohl, Volunteer Coordinator, Butterfly Pavilion

The Butterfly Pavilion is an interactive, educational facility featuring live collections of butterflies and insects. Its mission combines science education with hands-on activities to teach visitors about invertebrates, science, and conservation. Prior to this initiative, the Butterfly Pavilion had a volunteer program, with opportunities for special events volunteers and exhibit specialists, as well as seasonal volunteers who were recruited to work seasonally in the Pavilion's indoor and outdoor gardens. When the Butterfly Pavilion signed on with the Boomer Volunteer Engagement program, staff was busy preparing for their first-ever traveling exhibition, "Tropical Odyssey," for which they planned to recruit at least 25 temporary exhibition volunteers, a six-month commitment. This was an entirely new endeavor for the Butterfly Pavilion and staff knew that it would take a different approach to volunteer recruitment to be successful. The organization's volunteer coordination staff and leadership were interested in partnering with a facilitator to develop a volunteer engagement pilot that would successfully engage Boomers as temporary exhibit volunteers as they believed that the short-term nature of the temporary exhibition would be appealing to Boomers as would the exhibit's conservation-related message.

The Butterfly Pavilion developed a Task Force of both staff and volunteers who learned about Boomer volunteer characteristics, designed position descriptions that would be Boomer-friendly, updated the volunteer application to include a section on skills, and developed a targeted marketing plan. The team moved quickly and efficiently, and, within 4 months of launching the Task Force, the Butterfly Pavilion had recruited 25 new temporary exhibit volunteers. Of the 25 exhibit volunteers, roughly half were new volunteers to the organization and the other half were existing volunteers, many of whom had assumed the same volunteer role for many years, but were attracted to this new opportunity to do something different. Once the temporary exhibition closed, many of the new volunteers have stayed on, including one who has negotiated a new role that utilizes her skills in art and education to develop hands-on materials for the Butterfly Room.

Many of the strategies developed through the pilot project have been incorporated into the Butterfly Pavilion's ongoing volunteer cultivation practices. Kris Pohl, Volunteer Coordinator, explains, "In the past, volunteers came to us, and through this program we have become more intentional and strategic. I now have a very detailed marketing plan." She continues to use the interview techniques employed through the pilot project, providing more customized tours and interviews to interested Boomers and focusing on the options available and how their skills could fit in.

Most significant was the long term impact of the Task Force itself. The opportunity for staff and volunteers on the Task Force to collaborate and jointly explore solutions to the organization's needs was enlightening and exciting. The Butterfly Pavilion will be sustaining a group of volunteer leaders as a leadership team advising on volunteer engagement issues into the future.

STEPPING STONES
The Value of being Nimble

When you change your mindset and think more about what volunteers need and want to offer you, rather than a preconceived notion of what you need, you exponentially increase your chances of success. —Phyllis Adler, Executive Director, Stepping Stones

Stepping Stones is a Jewish outreach organization that supports and educates interfaith families and connects interfaith and unaffiliated families to Judaism. Part of its mission is to serve as a central resource center for outreach and to offer fun, interactive, and educational opportunities for intermarried couples and families to explore Jewish life. At the time that Stepping Stones engaged a volunteer to facilitate a volunteer engagement initiative, the organization had no volunteers other than Board members. The hope was for staff to learn volunteer engagement skills by implementing one small pilot project using volunteers.

Working with the facilitator, Stepping Stones developed a Task Force consisting of the executive director, a marketing staff member, and a small group of volunteers including two Board members and an intern from a local graduate school of social work. After assessing their organizational needs, team members identified a pilot project. The goal was to engage volunteers to help develop a new revenue stream through a sponsorship program. Stepping Stones was soon to launch an online resource: An interactive map detailing community resources in its metropolitan area. The Task Force hoped to engage a volunteer sales force to solicit community businesses for sponsorships of this online resource. The Task Force developed a Work Plan, established a timeline, drafted position descriptions, and prepared to cultivate volunteers. As they proceeded, they encountered a challenging delay: Before soliciting sponsors, the organization still had legal and financial logistics to confirm before officially launching a sponsorship program. In the meantime, they had a committed, invested Task Force of volunteers and staff who had been learning and utilizing new skills in volunteer engagement. They had a comprehensive list of potential projects, in addition to the original idea of the volunteer sales force. So, instead of disbanding the Task Force and waiting until the website issues were resolved, they applied those skills and practices to other opportunities.

Since the pilot program, Stepping Stones staff members have leveraged all that they learned and, even though they were unable to complete their original Work Plan within the intended timeline, they took advantage of the momentum and built capacity in other ways. According to the Stepping Stones executive director, in a period of six months, they went from zero volunteers to over 40 volunteers, including program alumni and community members who are now helping with program planning and recruitment of new program participants. They have a volunteer who works professionally as an internet marketing specialist sharing her technological knowledge to help advance the original project. The staff is explicit in their commitment to aligning the interests and skills of potential volunteers with key capacity-building areas, including donor development, volunteer cultivation, marketing, and leadership development.

CASE STUDY

METRO VOLUNTEERS
Engaging Volunteer Leaders to Strengthen the Community's Nonprofits

In a time when all nonprofits are facing economic challenges and increased demand for services, this program provides a strategic solution. Through this model of partnering professional and volunteer staff, Metro Volunteers has developed and launched several new programs that help local nonprofits recognize and utilize volunteers as a critical resource in addressing societal needs. —Kristy Judd, Executive Director, Metro Volunteers

Metro Volunteers is a volunteer center dedicated to its mission of "mobilizing and cultivating volunteers as a vital force in our community." The organization serves both volunteers and other agencies by helping individuals, families, and corporate and community groups find volunteer opportunities while also providing programs to nonprofits to help strengthen their leadership and volunteer management practices. With the wave of Baby Boomers entering the volunteer force, Metro Volunteers leadership was very interested in exploring ways to deploy Baby Boomers into rewarding volunteer opportunities in the community while also preparing local nonprofits with the tools they would need to meaningfully engage these Boomer volunteers. This interest, combined with its proven track record for training programs, positioned Metro Volunteers well to pilot a new program that would address these emerging needs.

The idea was simple: Offer local nonprofits a trained facilitator who would guide their organization through the process of Boomer volunteer engagement (using the book **Boomer Volunteer Engagement** as the textbook), by convening a task force, providing coaching, sharing tools, and holding the team accountable. Due to economic pressures that most nonprofits faced during this time period, Metro Volunteers was not in a position to hire a new staff person to develop such a program. So, Metro Volunteers Executive Director Kristy Judd took this opportunity to engage experienced Baby Boomers and empowered them to lead and manage an initiative designed to address some of these issues. Those volunteers included retired nonprofit executive director Steve Norris, retired corporate executive Hannah Levy, and retired volunteer coordinator and part-time consultant Sandie Eichberg. Those three individuals formed an Operations Team that worked closely with Judd and with us, as our firm provided technical assistance and developed the tools for use in the program. While we provided the content, the Operations Team developed a marketing plan to recruit volunteers and nonprofits, conducted interviews and made selections, deployed the facilitators to the nonprofits, managed the communications, and tracked the Work Plan for the program overall. While allowing other Metro Volunteers staff to focus on fulfilling their strategic priorities and stewarding other critical initiatives, the Operations Team developed a program that successfully introduced five local nonprofit organizations to the power and potential of Boomer volunteer engagement and did so while modeling the collaborative approach themselves. Throughout, Kristy Judd and our team provided support to the Operations Team in the form of technical assistance and resources, and the Operations Team implemented the program overall.

Following the initial 12-month program (six months of program development, including facilitator recruitment and training and then six months of supporting the facilitators while they were working with their nonprofit organizations), the Operations Team continues to thrive. They have completed a hearty evaluation of the project, developed a plan to sustain the program within Metro Volunteers, recruited new non-profits to participate, and deployed facilitators to those organizations. The program launched in February 2010, and is called Volunteers with Impact and Purpose (VIP Program). Thanks to this program and the volunteer-led Operations Team, Metro Volunteers is now positioned to provide an invaluable resource to its community and strengthen local nonprofits at the same time.

HOW TO USE THIS BOOK

This Tool Kit presents a detailed timeline and all the tools needed for engaging co-facilitators to guide your organization through a Boomer Volunteer Engagement Initiative. As a complement to the book *Boomer Volunteer Engagement*, the Tool Kit refers frequently to content and exercises in Boomer Volunteer Engagement. For ease of navigation, we have duplicated all of the tools referenced from the book in this Tool Kit, so you can easily find them within this one resource. The book does contain critical information that we have not replicated here, including, for example, background content, a glossary, and bibliography.

This Tool Kit is written as a detailed timeline spanning eight months, with month-by-month instructions including intended outcomes, meeting agendas, discussion guides, and more. There are eight modules, each with detailed guidelines on how to co-facilitate a volunteer engagement initiative. An Epilogue follows, focusing on how recent trends in volunteerism make this an unprecedented time to engage volunteers as leaders of new initiatives and as partners in fulfilling organizational mission. Modules 2 through 8 have a common structure with sections identified by icons.

The calendar icon suggests when in the timeline each module's activities should be implemented.

KEY OUTCOMES 🔍

Each module begins with key outcomes.

Related Material in
Boomer Volunteer Engagement

The relevant material from the book ***Boomer Volunteer Engagement, Collaborate Today, Thrive Tomorrow*** is highlighted here for easy reference.

[THE FRAMEWORK]

We define the contextual background for each month's work.

⚙ TOOLS

This is an exercise or list of exercises to be used in this module

✔ MAKING IT HAPPEN

Steps and exercises are provided in this section.

⚙ TOOL REVIEW

An overview of the exercise, including what it is, why it is important, and how to use it.

TASK FORCE PROGRESS REPORT

Sections conclude with a tool for the Task Force to use to track progress.

Each module relates to approximately one month of activities. Please note that the timeline is a suggestion, based on our experience that this work can be achieved with tangible results over an eight-month period. You should adapt the timeline to the reality and schedule of your organization. Modules 1 and 2 will likely take two months and focus on cultivating co-facilitators and Task Force members, as well as giving the co-facilitators time to prepare. Modules 3 through 8 include the tools that co-facilitators will need to successfully facilitate 6 Task Force Work Sessions. In addition to the elements listed above (i.e. Key Outcomes, The Framework, etc.), these modules include a detailed agenda for each Task Force Work Session. The Agendas include the following helpful suggestions and resources:

PARTICIPANTS

We suggest who should attend the Work Session for best results.

MEETING LENGTH

A recommended timeframe for the meeting in order to ensure there is sufficient time to complete the agenda.

PREP WORK

The Task Force should complete this work prior to the Task Force Work Session.

 **DISCUSSION GUIDE**   Questions and speaking points to focus the Task Force on issues, tasks, and implementation during the Work Sessions.

All of the exercises included in the book *Boomer Volunteer Engagement* are available as downloadable PDFs at www.BoomerVolunteerEngagement.org. Some are interactive PDF forms with fillable fields and can be saved on your drive. This Tool Kit is available both as hardcopy and as an eBook. If you are using an eBook, note that you can print exercises one at a time off of the eBook. To order *Boomer Volunteer Engagement: Collaborate Today, Thrive Tomorrow* or the print or digital version of the Tool Kit, visit www.BoomerVolunteerEngagement.org.

NOTES & IDEAS

Planning and Cultivation

Getting the Right People at the Table

KEY OUTCOMES

1. Organizational leadership will clearly understand the powerful outcomes of a Boomer Volunteer Engagement Initiative and will communicate their support through a signed resolution of support.

2. Co-facilitators will be cultivated to lead the initiative.

3. A list of potential Task Force members will be generated and a cultivation plan will be developed.

Related Material in *Boomer Volunteer Engagement*:

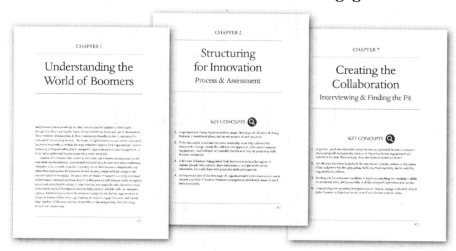

[THE FRAMEWORK]

Re-engineering volunteer management into volunteer engagement takes resources, time, and – most importantly – commitment…. For a nonprofit to move from a volunteer management model to one that engages Boomers for the skills and passions they have to offer, the leadership of the organization must fully embrace the change. —(Page 26, ***Boomer Volunteer Engagement***)

The first two months of this endeavor lay the foundation for its ultimate success. This initial period focuses on three main activities: securing leadership support, cultivating effective facilitators, and identifying potential Task Force members. All of these efforts reflect the importance of securing support and involvement of key stakeholders. Chapter 2 of the book explores the theory behind organizational change and the rationale for gaining the support of the nonprofit executive. It also details the role of the Boomer Volunteer Engagement Task Force – which is charged with creating the vision for the Boomer Volunteer Engagement Initiative, shepherding the process, and monitoring outcomes. Cultivating a volunteer and staff member to work in partnership as co-facilitators of this process enhances the effort by:

- Providing support and guidance for the process.
- Keeping the process moving forward.
- Providing information and accountability to the Task Force.
- Modeling the power of staff/volunteer collaboration from the start.

The following tools will help you secure leadership support, cultivate skilled co-facilitators, and invite effective members onto your Boomer Volunteer Engagement Task Force.

⚙⚙ TOOLS

- Volunteer Engagement Timeline
- Overview for Organizational Leaders
- Organizational Commitment and Expectations
- Resolution in Support of Boomer Volunteer Engagement Initiative
- Co-Facilitator Position Description
- Co-Facilitator Recruitment Messages
- Staff Co-Facilitator Selection Checklist
- Response Letter to Volunteer Co-Facilitator Candidates
- Refusal Letter to Volunteer Co-Facilitator Candidates
- Co-Facilitator Addendum to Standard Volunteer Application
- Interview Checklist for Volunteer Co-Facilitator Candidates
- Volunteer Co-Facilitator Selection Matrix
- Boomer Volunteer Engagement Task Force Brainstorm Exercise
- Task Force Member Position Description
- Task Force Recruitment Messages

The volunteer engagement process can be achieved in approximately eight months (two months of preparation and six months of pilot development and implementation). The process can be longer, depending on the organization's calendar and the details of the pilot project – but it is important to note that substantial results can be achieved in just an eight-month period.

Following is a **Step-by-Step Timeline for Nonprofits** to use the materials contained in this Tool Kit. This is your itinerary for a journey that is sure to bring your organization to new heights of community engagement and mission-fulfillment.

Months 1 and 2 – Gaining Support and Recruiting Co-Facilitators

- Gain Board support for the project by presenting the **Volunteer Engagement Timeline**, the **Overview for Organizational Leaders**, and the **Organizational Commitment and Expectations** to them.
- Demonstrate Board commitment to the volunteer engagement initiative by having the Board sign the **Resolution in Support of Boomer Volunteer Engagement Initiative** to show support of the endeavor.
- Identify staff members who could be a successful and effective staff Co-Facilitator by referring to the **Co-Facilitator Position Description** and using the **Staff Co-Facilitator Selection Checklist**. Select a staff member to serve as the staff Co-Facilitator for the project.
- Involve the staff co-facilitator where possible and cultivate and engage a volunteer co-facilitator for the project, using the **Co-Facilitator Position Description** and the **Co-Facilitator Recruitment Messages** to help broadcast the opportunity to your constituents and beyond.
- Once you have received indications of interest from potential volunteer candidates, send the **Letter to Volunteer Co-Facilitator Candidates**, along with the **Position Description, Project Timeline**, and **Co-Facilitator Addendum to Standard Volunteer Application**.
- Refer to the **Interview Checklist for Volunteer Co-Facilitator Candidates** to guide the interview conversation and refer to Chapter 7 in the book, *Boomer Volunteer Engagement*, for tips on interviewing.

- Complete the **Volunteer Co-Facilitator Selection Matrix** during the interviews and then refer to it when making your selection of co-facilitator candidates. Offer the position to two candidates who will make the best team of co-facilitators.
- In the meantime, complete the **Boomer Volunteer Engagement Task Force Brainstorm Exercise** in order to generate a list of potential Task Force members.
- Refer to the **Task Force Member Position Description** and use the **Task Force Recruitment Messages** to help broadcast the opportunity to your constituents and beyond.

Volunteer Engagement Timeline

WHAT: This Timeline is an overview for use in planning and discussions with non-profit leaders about supporting this initiative. It is based on a schedule of two months of preparation and readiness, followed by six months of Task Force work, totaling eight months.

WHY: It will help establish realistic expectations and ensure sufficient resources, including human resources, are allocated to ensure success.

HOW: Use this document as a resource during personal meetings with nonprofit leaders and prepare to leave it with them. Share this document with the Task Force later on as a resource for identifying milestones.

The volunteer engagement process can be achieved in approximately eight months (two months of preparation and six months of pilot development and implementation). The process can be longer, depending on the organization's calendar and the details of the pilot project – but it is important to note that substantial results can be achieved in just an eight-month period.

Month 1: Gaining Support and Recruiting Co-Facilitators
- Board review and commitment of support for volunteer engagement initiative.
- Cultivation and selection of a Staff and a Volunteer co-facilitator.

Month 2: Co-Facilitator Preparation and Task Force Cultivation
- Co-facilitator preparation and planning.
- Task Force establishment.
- Initial communication from co-facilitators to the Task Force members.

Month 3: Task Force Work Session 1 – Parts A and B: Making the Case for Volunteer Engagement and Creating a Culture of Volunteer Engagement
- Task Force launch.
- Case Statement development.
- Pilot Project identification.

Month 4: Task Force Work Session 2 – Creating Volunteer Opportunities
- Project selection and Work Plan finalized.
- Volunteer position descriptions developed.

Month 5: Task Force Work Session 3 – Interviewing, Negotiation, and Support
- New position descriptions marketed.
- Interviews planned and conducted.
- New volunteers placed in positions.

Month 6: Task Force Work Session 4 – Launching the Pilot and Tracking Progress
- Pilot project launched.
- Volunteers supported in their new roles.

Month 7: Task Force Work Session 5 – Tracking Progress and Preparing to Wrap-Up
- Pilot project continues.
- Progress tracked and Work Plan updated.

Month 8: Task Force Work Session 6 – Documenting the Program and Sustaining the Culture
- Pilot results documented.
- Successes shared.
- Next steps mapped out.

Overview for Organizational Leaders

WHAT: This template is the basis for discussions within your nonprofit organization.

WHY: It will help garner support for the endeavor, which is crucial to establish volunteer engagement as a strategic priority, to ensure the initiative has ample support, to hold those involved accountable, and to establish a culture in which experimentation is encouraged.

HOW: Use this document as a script for a personal meeting, adapt it as a background document to leave with leaders of your nonprofit, and use it as the basis for a volunteer engagement discussion at an organizational Board meeting.

Boomer Volunteer Engagement is an initiative designed to help our organization build its capacity and benefit from the skills and talents of Boomer volunteers. Imagine a world in which our nonprofit has the resources it needs to serve more clients, deliver more programs, strengthen our staff, and increase our financial stability – no matter the economic climate.

Boomers are redefining volunteerism and, in the process, transforming volunteerism. Launching a volunteer engagement initiative will help our organization to expand our mission-oriented capacity by engaging experienced Baby Boomer volunteers to partner with staff as co-facilitators in a structured process of innovation. There is no better time than now to shift from a culture of traditional volunteer management to a collaborative model of volunteer engagement. Engaging Boomer volunteers is a powerful way to mobilize a generation over 78 million strong, to bring them into a relationship with our mission, and to use their skills and passions to collaboratively build our capacity to serve clients, deliver programs, and to build skills in volunteer engagement that will resonate with not only Boomers, but also with the generations that follow.

Through this innovative initiative, our organization can gain the competencies to make the shift to a volunteer model in which Boomer volunteers will help us reach well beyond what staff alone can accomplish. Working with skilled facilitators (including a current staff or Board member from the organization working in tandem with an experienced volunteer), we will follow the step-by-step process for organizational capacity-building outlined in the book *Boomer Volunteer Engagement: Collaborate Today, Thrive Tomorrow*. Together, the book and this Tool Kit provides us with everything we need to engage Boomer volunteers and benefit from their skills, passions, and experience.

Benefits and Outcomes

By participating in this endeavor, we can expect the following outcomes and benefits:

- Current and relevant research on Baby Boomers.
- Skilled co-facilitators to guide us through a proven, step-by-step process for Boomer Volunteer Engagement.
- An array of volunteer engagement exercises and templates to apply to a new or existing project that fits our organization's priorities.
- The skills and passions of Baby Boomer volunteers and their service as consultants, coaches, mentors, experts, designers, writers, and more to help our organization build capacity to fulfill its mission.
- Increased organizational capacity through accessing skills and resources from within our existing circles of influence so that we can survive and thrive.

Volunteers are not a program... they are a business decision.
Volunteer engagement is the #1 organizational strategy for the new economy.
—Metro Volunteers

Organizational Commitment and Expectations

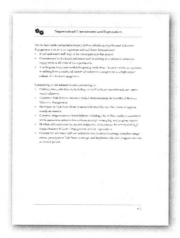

WHAT: This template is the basis for discussions with organizational leadership.

WHY: It will help establish realistic expectations and ensure sufficient resources, including human resources, are allocated to ensure success.

HOW: Use this document as a resource during meetings with organizational leadership, as the basis of team and management meetings, and as a resource to leave with key staff and leaders for further consideration.

For the best results and greatest impact, before embarking on a Boomer Volunteer Engagement endeavor, an organization should have demonstrated:

- Board and senior staff support for participation in this project.
- Commitment by the Board and senior staff to shifting to a culture of volunteer engagement at all levels of the organization.
- A willingness to try new models for getting work done – in other words, an openness to shifting from a traditional culture of volunteer management to a high-impact culture of volunteer engagement.

Committing to this initiative means committing to:

- Cultivate two co-facilitators, including one staff or Board member and one experienced volunteer.
- Convene a Task Force to oversee a project demonstrating the benefits of Boomer Volunteer Engagement.
- Participate in Task Force Work Sessions held monthly over the course of approximately six months.
- Complete assignments in a timely fashion, including a Work Plan, readiness assessment, needs assessment, position descriptions, strategic messaging, and progress reports.
- Develop and implement one project designed to demonstrate the potential of high-impact Boomer Volunteer Engagement in their organization.
- Commit the necessary staff and volunteer time to attend trainings, complete assignments, participate in Task Force meetings, and implement the pilot program over the six-month period.

Resolution in Support of Boomer Volunteer Engagement Initiative

WHAT: This is a Resolution of Support to be reviewed and signed by the organization's Board of Directors as a sign of support for establishing a Task Force and having dedicated co-facilitators to demonstrate the power and potential of Boomer Volunteer Engagement.

WHY: Board support for a Boomer Volunteer Engagement Initiative is important. The Board's written commitment helps to ensure that resources are allocated appropriately, demonstrates that volunteer engagement is an important, enterprise-wide strategy, and builds champions for the effort amongst organizational leaders.

HOW: Make a presentation to the Board about Boomer Volunteer Engagement using the timeline, overview, and commitment and expectations documents, then introduce this resolution for discussion and signatures. Preparing a case statement for Boomer Volunteer Engagement prior to the meeting may be helpful for discussion. You can find a template for a case statement in Chapter 5 of the book. Signing this resolution – or a version customized to your organization – indicates Board and organizational leadership commitment to support the initiative.

⚙⚙ Resolution in Support of Boomer Volunteer Engagement Initiative

The Board of Trustees of _____ recognizes the importance and potential of Boomer Volunteer Engagement as a strategy to build our organizational capacity and to fulfill our mission, and hereby commits to full support of this volunteer engagement initiative.

We pledge to support the program by having one staff and one volunteer from our organization co-facilitate a Task Force. We will support both staff and volunteer members of this Task Force as they learn, contribute to project development and performance measurement, and share best practices with other staff and volunteers.

We further pledge to support the initiative and the Task Force's efforts to complete assignments, implement a pilot program, evaluate progress, and work with their co-facilitators throughout this eight-month endeavor. We will allocate the tools, technology, best practices, and program evaluation needed for the success of the pilot and for the process of determining which elements of the pilot can be sustained or adapted for the future.

Finally, we will make ourselves available throughout the pilot program to observe, support, and share results with the greater community.

_____   _____
Board President   Date

Other Board Signatures:

_____

_____

_____

_____

_____
                                                                      Date

Co-Facilitator Position Description

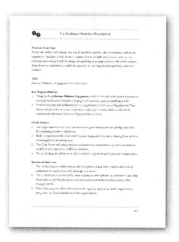

WHAT: A position description details the role and responsibilities of the co-facilitators and is the basis for cultivation, selection, and support of these individuals.

WHY: A carefully considered, well-written volunteer position description is the reference point for negotiation, support, accountability, and evaluation. Therefore it is key to the co-facilitators' success.

HOW: Use this position description to help identify potential co-facilitators, to clarify the co-facilitator's role when cultivating and negotiating with co-facilitator candidates, and to serve as a point of reference throughout the project as organizational leadership provides support to the co-facilitators and holds them accountable.

Co-Facilitator Position Description

Position Overview

These two skilled individuals, one a staff member and the other a volunteer, will work together to facilitate a Task Force (comprised of both staff and volunteers from our organization) charged with learning and applying new approaches to effectively engage Baby Boomer volunteers to build the capacity of our organization and help fulfill our mission.

Title

Boomer Volunteer Engagement Co-Facilitator

Key Responsibilities

1. Using the book *Boomer Volunteer Engagement* and this Tool Kit as the primary resources, learn about Boomer Volunteer Engagement and this capacity-building model.
2. Provide training and facilitation to this organization's Volunteer Engagement Task Force and provide resources, motivation, and support in its effort to effectively implement a Boomer Volunteer Engagement Initiative.

Initial Impact

1. Our organization's staff and volunteers will gain measurable knowledge and skills for engaging Boomer volunteers.
2. Skilled, experienced Boomers will become engaged volunteers, sharing their skills in meaningful and satisfying ways.
3. The Task Force will utilize Boomer volunteers to implement a project that demonstrably builds capacity to fulfill our mission.
4. The co-facilitators will serve as role models for high level staff/volunteer collaboration.

Sustained Outcome

1. The co-facilitators' collaboration will be replicated and others will be able to lead additional initiatives that fulfill strategic priorities.
2. The co-facilitators or some of the new volunteers will replicate the volunteer leadership demonstrated by this pilot process to lead additional initiatives that address other strategic needs.
3. The co-facilitators will be able to provide ongoing support to other departments, programs, or future initiatives of this organization.

Training

Co-facilitators will utilize the book *Boomer Volunteer Engagement* in combination with this Tool Kit, which includes detailed meeting agendas, exercises and worksheets for the Task Force, timelines, progress reports, and evaluation tools.

Support

Co-facilitators will have the support of organizational leaders for resources needed to complete the initiative and as advocates for the endeavor as a whole. They will be our champions in the organization.

Commitment

Co-facilitators are expected to be available for a period of at least eight months, including one to two months of preparation followed by six months of facilitation. The monthly commitment would include facilitation of at least one 2-hour meeting, plus preparation and follow up by email or telephone to keep the Task Force on track and accountable for assignments and deliverables.

Qualifications

- Belief in – and passion for – the potential of volunteer engagement to help nonprofits fulfill their dreams.
- Communication skills, both oral and written.
- Public speaking and/or teaching experience.
- Facilitation and/or coaching experience.
- Experience working in staff/volunteer collaborations, whether as the staff member or as the volunteer.
- Ability to work on a two-person team and job-share responsibilities, as well as the ability to lead teams.
- Experience in organizational development and/or nonprofit management a bonus.

Benefits

- The opportunity to truly make a long-lasting difference for our organization by demonstrating the power of skills-based volunteer engagement.
- The opportunity to participate in and help shape an innovative model for nonprofit capacity-building.
- Gaining new skills in facilitation and experience in professional coaching.

Co-Facilitator Recruitment Messages

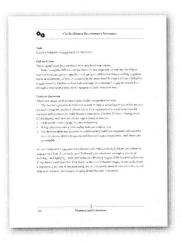

WHAT: This is a resource of compelling and clear messages to be used for cultivating co-facilitators.

WHY: All marketing – including marketing to cultivate volunteers – is more effective if the message is clear and strategically crafted. This is especially true when seeking high-impact volunteers, as Boomers and the generations that follow are motivated by knowing the impact they could have if they took on this role.

HOW: Customize the following blurbs to help you cultivate qualified candidates for your co-facilitator positions. These blurbs can be used on the organization's website, employee communications, and newsletters, with online volunteer search engines (such as VolunteerMatch.org), and as scripts for personal conversations.

Title

Boomer Volunteer Engagement Co-Facilitator

Call to Action

This is a good length for a website ad or an inset box in a newsletter.

Make a tangible difference in the future of our organization and directly help us reach beyond our current capacity – and use your skills in teaching, coaching, organizational development, or human resources at the same time! Become a Boomer Volunteer Engagement Co-Facilitator, then train and support a volunteer engagement task force through a step-by-step process of engaging volunteers in new ways.

Position Overview

Where more detail can be printed or posted online, use position overview.

The Boomer generation continues to seek to leave a social legacy and, in the process, is transforming the world of volunteerism. Our organization is ready to harness the energies and talents of the Baby Boomer generation. Boomer Volunteer Engagement Co-Facilitators will have the unique opportunity to directly:

- Help us effectively engage Boomer volunteers;
- Bring volunteers into a relationship with our mission; and
- Use Boomer skills and passions to collaboratively build our organizational capacity to serve clients, deliver programs, and have an impact beyond what staff alone can accomplish.

Boomer Volunteer Engagement Facilitators will collaboratively facilitate our volunteer engagement Task Force made up of both staff and volunteers through a process of learning – and applying – new approaches to effectively engage Baby Boomer volunteers. Co-facilitators will train this Task Force on Boomer Volunteer Engagement, co-facilitate a step-by-step process of implementing one pilot program using Boomer volunteers, and help us to measure the impacts of using skilled Boomer volunteers.

Personal Invitation

If you already know of good candidates within your midst, identify the best person to approach them and use this script as a basis for the personal invitation.

We value your skills and the way that you can envision a bigger future for our organization. We invite you to participate with us as we launch an initiative to help us transform the way we work with volunteers in order to intentionally and effectively engage Baby Boomers and all the skills they have to offer. It will be some of the most important work we can do in our community.

We are asking you to consider using your skills in [insert: organizational development, teaching, nonprofit management… or the like] to become one of two Boomer Volunteer Engagement Co-Facilitators. Co-facilitators will guide a Task Force through a step-by-step process designed to help us shift from traditional volunteer management to volunteer engagement. You would provide training and facilitation and would receive support materials and a Facilitator's Tool Kit to help you. Can we set up a time to discuss the position description and see if this is a fit for you and for our organization?

Staff Co-Facilitator Selection Guide

WHAT: This list includes items that should be considered when selecting a staff co-facilitator for the volunteer engagement initiative.

WHY: Selecting the staff co-facilitator is a strategic decision and should be made carefully and intentionally. Selecting an individual who not only has the skills and availability, but also has the influence, respect, and/or status will dramatically increase the chances for success.

HOW: Use this selection guide in combination with the Co-Facilitator Position Description to brainstorm which staff members could be a successful co-facilitator for the process. Review all possible staff co-facilitators against this list and refer to it as you meet with potential co-facilitators. You can also refer to the Volunteer Co-Facilitator Interview Checklist as a reference for in-person conversations with potential staff co-facilitators.

The following traits are important characteristics to have in a staff co-facilitator. Each trait is key to ensuring that the co-facilitator can successfully collaborate, facilitate, problem-solve, and champion volunteer engagement throughout the organization.

The staff co-facilitator should have:

- ✓ Passionate belief in the potential and power of volunteer engagement
- ✓ Previous experience as a facilitator
- ✓ Understanding of facilitation
- ✓ Understanding of the organization
- ✓ Demonstrated project management skills
- ✓ Problem solving skills
- ✓ Motivational skills
- ✓ Demonstrated ability to collaborate
- ✓ Availability within schedule and workload to commit fully to completing this initiative
- ✓ Overall fit with the other Co-Facilitator
- ✓ Demonstrated follow-through
- ✓ Respect from peers

TIP: Consider how to strategically select an individual whose experience, influence, and/or position in the organization will help leverage this endeavor for success. The Volunteer Engagement Professional in your organization (e.g. Volunteer Coordinator, Director of Volunteer Services) may or may not be the person to fulfill this role. That individual may not have the time, experience, or position in the organization to be the most effective co-facilitator, but that individual should certainly be a member of the Task Force. This is an opportunity to look beyond the obvious choice and think strategically about how to get key stakeholders around this table, whether as the co-facilitator or as a Task Force Member.

Response Letter to Volunteer Co-Facilitator Candidates

WHAT: This follow-up letter template is a response to individuals who respond to the strategic messages calling for a volunteer to be a co-facilitator.

WHY: Formal follow-up establishes that the organization is serious and professional and it provides important information that will help candidates determine whether they are a good fit for the position. By doing so, you will be more likely to only interview candidates whose interests, skills, and availability match the expectations and responsibilities of the position.

HOW: Customize this text and use it as the base of a letter or email to follow up on a candidate's expression of interest and to schedule an interview. This text is for use with candidates who are qualified for the position and whom you wish to interview.

Dear [Insert Name],

It was a pleasure to speak with you recently about the possibility of your becoming one of our two Boomer Volunteer Engagement co-facilitators. This initiative is a unique opportunity to make a tangible difference in the future of our organization by using your skills in teaching, coaching, and organizational development. [personalize]

As a Boomer Volunteer Engagement Co-Facilitator, you would work in partnership with the staff co-facilitator to train and support our Task Force through a step-by-step process designed to help us build organizational capacity through engaging skilled Boomer volunteers. You would directly:

- Help our Task Force better understand the foundation of Boomer Volunteer Engagement;
- Guide the selection of a pilot project to demonstrate the power of volunteer engagement;
- Help our organization effectively engage Boomer volunteers as part of this pilot project; and
- Use Boomer skills and passions to collaboratively build our organizational capacity to serve clients and deliver programs.

As we discussed, this initiative will be some of the most important work we can do in our community. I have enclosed a copy of the Co-Facilitator Position Description for your information.

Please review the Position Description. I will contact you shortly to follow up and discuss whether this is a fit for you. If so, we will schedule an interview during which we can discuss this opportunity further. In the meantime, feel free to contact me with any questions.

Thank you.

Signature
Title

Refusal Letter to Volunteer Co-Facilitator Candidates

WHAT: This follow-up letter template is a response to volunteers who have been interviewed and have not been selected for the position of Volunteer Co-Facilitator.

WHY: Sending a follow-up letter maintains a written record of the communication and gives the opportunity to thank the individual for investing the time in being interviewed and considering the position. Courteous, clear communications can maintain a positive relationship with the individual and keep options open for future volunteer opportunities that may be a better fit.

HOW: Customize this text and use it as the base of a letter or email to follow up on a candidate's application.

Dear [Insert Name],

It was a pleasure to speak with you recently about the Boomer Volunteer Engagement Co-Facilitator position. Based on the unique needs of this position, we do not believe that it is a good fit for your skills and experience. We appreciate your interest and thank you for taking the time to talk with us about this opportunity.

We will keep your information on file and will certainly keep you in mind as we develop new volunteer opportunities. If there are other areas of interest to you, please let us know and we can discuss those that might be a better fit for your interests.

Thank you,

Signature
Title

Co-Facilitator Addendum to Standard Volunteer Application

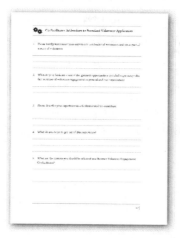

WHAT: This is an addendum to your organization's standard volunteer application with questions specific to the co-facilitator position.

WHY: Having a candidate complete these questions provides information to both you and the candidate that will help determine whether this position is a good fit for that individual's skills, interests, and availability.

HOW: Append this to your standard organizational volunteer application forms and ensure that all co-facilitator applicants complete this section as well.

Co-Facilitator Addendum to Standard Volunteer Application

1. Please briefly summarize your experience as a leader of volunteers and/or as part of a team of volunteers.

2. What do you think are some of the greatest opportunities and challenges nonprofits face in terms of volunteer engagement in general and our organization?

3. Please describe your experience as a facilitator and/or consultant.

4. What do you hope to get out of this experience?

5. What are the reasons you should be selected as a Boomer Volunteer Engagement Co-Facilitator?

Interview Checklist for Volunteer Co-Facilitator Candidates

WHAT: This list includes items that should be discussed during a telephone or face-to-face conversation after the candidate completes and submits a volunteer co-facilitator application.

WHY: A telephone or face-to-face interview with candidates for the volunteer co-facilitator position is an important part of the selection process – even if the candidates are known to the organization. The interview creates an opportunity to identify candidates' priorities and lets them know the goals, mission, vision, and culture of the organization.

HOW: Use this checklist as you plan your interviews of co-facilitator candidates and refer to this list throughout the interview to ensure you address these issues.

Application Review

- Review of candidate's application.
- Request for clarification or additional information on any of the questions as applicable.

Questions

- Why are you interested in this position?
- Please define the facilitation process. What is most challenging for you and why?
- In your previous work as a facilitator and/or trainer, what are three of your greatest achievements? And why?
- Imagine that members of your Task Force are very invested in the Boomer Volunteer Engagement Initiative, but encounter a lot of staff resistance to the change. What would you do?
- Describe a situation in which you were leading a team or facilitating a group in which the participants were not fulfilling their commitments to the process – whether it be completing assignments, showing up, participating fully, etc. How did you handle it? If you haven't experienced this before, how would you handle it if you did face it?
- Tell us about the most difficult group that you have worked with. What did you learn from this experience? What would you do differently next time?

Volunteer's Questions

- Do you have questions about this initiative and your potential role in it?
- Do you have any other questions?

Final Notes

- Inform of notification process.

TOOL REVIEW

 Volunteer Co-Facilitator Selection Matrix

WHAT: This is a scoring rubric to be used by the interviewers to compare candidates for the volunteer co-facilitator position.

WHY: A matrix helps to ensure that candidates are judged with some objectivity and that all interviewers are considering the same competencies and can compare their assessments.

HOW: Ensure that each interviewer is familiar with the position description, the candidate's application, and this form. Have each interviewer complete this form, listing each interviewee in a different column. In this way, candidates can be compared to other candidates and multiple interviewers can systematically compare their assessments of the candidates.

Volunteer Co-Facilitator Selection Matrix

Instructions

1. Add candidates' names to the top row, one name per column.
2. Rate each candidate in each area, using a scale of 0 to 3, as follows:

   "0" = No experience or understanding

   "1" = Limited experience or understanding; could be stronger

   "2" = Sufficient experience or understanding

   "3" = Excellent experience or understanding
3. Use the ratings comparisons during the selection meeting.

	Candidates			
Experience w/ Volunteer Engagement				
Previous Experience as Facilitator				
Understanding of Facilitation				
Understanding of Nonprofit Sector				
Problem-Solving Skills				
Motivational Skills				
Personal Goals for Involvement				
Overall "Fit" with the other Co-Facilitator				
Professionalism				
Overall Impression				

Boomer Volunteer Engagement Task Force Brainstorm Exercise

WHAT: This is an exercise to help you generate a list of potential Task Force members.

WHY: An effective Task Force will include individuals from many of these diverse categories of skills and strengths. To ensure that the Task Force includes such members, it is helpful to take the time to consider these categories and brainstorm possible candidates for each.

HOW: Organizational leaders and, if the selection has been finalized, the co-facilitators should complete this exercise individually or as a group and then use their answers to generate a list of possible Task Force members.

Boomer Volunteer Engagement Task Force Brainstorm Exercise

1. Make a list of people already in your circle of influence from your Board, current volunteers, donors, clients and their families, partners, and vendors to invite into the planning and implementation process.

2. Of those individuals, whom would you describe as "visionary?" (Who has indicated an appreciation and understanding of the potential of Boomer volunteer engagement?)

3. Of those individuals, who are the strongest Connectors? (Who knows a lot of people? Is skilled at bringing people together? Has an extensive list of contacts and uses it?)

4. Of the individuals, who are the clear Mavens? (Which individuals have information about a topic of importance to this Task Force? Who collects information and likes to share it?)

5. Who from your list are the Salespeople? (Who is charismatic? Who is a persuader?)

6. What are the specific skills necessary for an effective Task Force for your organization? Who possesses this expertise and these talents?

Task Force Member Position Description

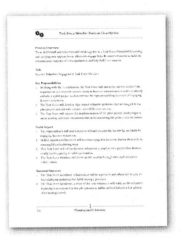

WHAT: A position description details the role and responsibilities of the Task Force members and is the basis for cultivation, selection, and support of these individuals.

WHY: A carefully considered, well-written volunteer position description is the reference point for negotiation, support, accountability, and evaluation. Therefore it is key to the Task Force success.

HOW: Use this position description along with the Brainstorm Exercise to help identify potential Task Force members, to clarify the Task Force's role when cultivating and negotiating with candidates for the Task Force, and to serve as a point of reference throughout the project as the co-facilitators hold the Task Force accountable.

Position Overview

These skilled staff and volunteers will work together as a Task Force charged with learning and applying new approaches to effectively engage Baby Boomer volunteers to build the organizational capacity of our organization and help fulfill our mission.

Title

Boomer Volunteer Engagement Task Force Member

Key Responsibilities

1. Working with the co-facilitators, the Task Force will assess the current needs of the organization and research current trends in Boomer volunteerism in order to identify and select a pilot project to demonstrate the capacity-building potential of engaging Boomer volunteers.
2. The Task Force will develop high-impact volunteer positions that are integral to the pilot project and cultivate volunteers to fill those positions.
3. The Task Force will oversee the implementation of the pilot project, track progress, assess success, and make recommendations for sustaining the project into the future.

Initial Impact

1. This organization's staff and volunteers will gain measurable knowledge and skills for engaging Boomer volunteers.
2. Skilled, experienced Boomers will become engaged volunteers, sharing their skills in meaningful and satisfying ways.
3. This Task Force will utilize Boomer volunteers to implement a project that demonstrably builds capacity to fulfill our mission.
4. The Task Force Members will serve as role models for high level staff/volunteer collaboration.

Sustained Outcome

1. The Task Force Members' collaboration will be replicated and others will be able to lead additional initiatives that fulfill strategic priorities.
2. The Task Force Members or some of the new volunteers will replicate the volunteer leadership demonstrated by this pilot process to lead additional initiatives that address other strategic needs.

3. The Task Force Members will be able to provide ongoing support to other departments, programs, or future initiatives of this organization.

Training

Task Force members will utilize the book *Boomer Volunteer Engagement* in combination with this Tool Kit, which includes detailed meeting agendas, exercises and worksheets, timelines, progress reports, and evaluation tools.

Support

The Task Force will be supported and guided by the co-facilitators.

Commitment

Task Force members are expected to be available for a period of at least six months. The monthly commitment would include at least one 2-hour meeting, plus completing select exercises in preparation or as follow up. Additionally, they will be responsible for implementing the pilot project or working with other staff and volunteers to ensure successful implementation. This could involve developing a Work Plan, drafting position descriptions, interviewing potential volunteers, selecting volunteers, tracking progress on the Work Plan, and evaluating success.

Qualifications

- Belief in – and passion for – the potential of volunteer engagement to help nonprofits fulfill their dreams.
- Communication skills, both oral and written.
- Project management experience.
- Experience working in staff/volunteer collaborations, whether as the staff member or as the volunteer.
- Experience in organizational development and/or nonprofit management a bonus.

Benefits

- The opportunity to truly make a difference for this organization by demonstrating the power of skills-based volunteer engagement.
- The opportunity to participate in and help shape an innovative model for nonprofit capacity-building.

Task Force Recruitment Messages

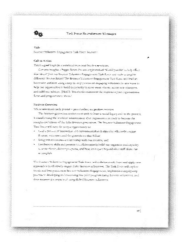

WHAT: This is a resource of compelling and clear messages to be used for cultivating Task Force members.

WHY: All marketing – including marketing to cultivate volunteers – is more effective if the message is clear and strategically crafted. This is especially true when seeking high-impact volunteers, as Boomers and the generations that follow are motivated by knowing the impact they could have if they took on this role.

HOW: Customize the following blurbs to help you cultivate qualified candidates for your Task Force memberships. These blurbs can be used on the organization's website, employee communications, and newsletters, with online volunteer search engines (such as VolunteerMatch.org), and as scripts for personal conversations. Chapter 2 of ***Boomer Volunteer Engagement*** details the importance of engaging a diverse group of individuals who are selected strategically to ensure that the team has relevant skills, connections, and styles.

Title
Boomer Volunteer Engagement Task Force Member

Call to Action
This is a good length for a website ad or an inset box in a newsletter.

Can you imagine a bigger future for our organization? Would you like to help effect that vision? Join our Boomer Volunteer Engagement Task Force and make a tangible difference for our future! The Boomer Volunteer Engagement Task Force will lead an innovative initiative using a step-by-step process of engaging volunteers in new ways to help our organization to build its capacity to serve more clients, access new resources, and fulfill our mission. [NOTE: You should customize the impacts to your organization's focus and programmatic focus.]

Position Overview
Where more detail can be printed or posted online, use position overview.

The Boomer generation continues to seek to leave a social legacy and, in the process, is transforming the world of volunteerism. Our organization is ready to harness the energies and talents of the Baby Boomer generation. The Boomer Volunteer Engagement Task Force will have the unique opportunity to:

- Lead a process of innovation and experimentation designed to effectively engage Boomer volunteers and the generations that follow;
- Bring volunteers into a relationship with our mission; and
- Use Boomer skills and passions to collaboratively build our organizational capacity to serve clients, deliver programs, and have an impact beyond what staff alone can accomplish.

The Boomer Volunteer Engagement Task Force will collaboratively learn and apply new approaches to effectively engage Baby Boomer volunteers. The Task Force will explore trends and best practices in Boomer Volunteer Engagement, implement a step-by-step process of developing and overseeing one pilot program using Boomer volunteers, and then measure the impacts of using skilled Boomer volunteers.

Personal Invitation

If you already know of good candidates within your midst, identify the best person to approach them and use this script as a basis for the personal invitation.

We value your skills and the way that you can envision a bigger future for our organization. We invite you to participate with us as we launch an initiative to help us transform the way we work with volunteers in order to intentionally and effectively engage Baby Boomers and all the skills they have to offer. It will be some of the most important work we can do for our organization.

We are asking you to consider using your skills in [insert: organizational development, teaching, nonprofit management... or the like] to become a member of the Boomer Volunteer Engagement Task Force. The Task Force will lead a step-by-step process designed to help us shift from traditional volunteer management to volunteer engagement. You would be part of a brand new collaborative team and receive materials and exercises to guide you through the process. Can we set up a time to discuss the position description and see if this is a fit for you and for our organization?

NOTES & IDEAS

Preparation

Preparing the Co-Facilitators and Cultivating the Task Force

KEY OUTCOMES 🔍

1. Co-facilitators will understand their roles and negotiate with each other for a productive division of labor throughout the course of the initiative.

2. The co-facilitators will be familiar with the Tool Kit, the process, and the model outlined in **Boomer Volunteer Engagement**.

3. A Task Force of diverse, skilled members is in place and ready to embark to develop a pilot of strategic volunteer engagement.

4. The co-facilitators will have established shared expectations and a positive working relationship with the Task Force through an introductory communication.

Related Material in *Boomer Volunteer Engagement*:

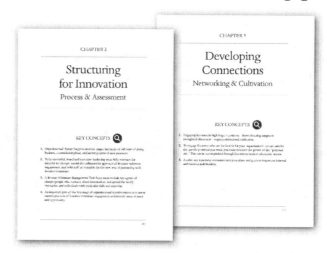

[THE FRAMEWORK]

As indicated in the Co-Facilitator Position Description, the role of the co-facilitators is to ensure that all members of the Task Force are comfortably and effectively involved in all aspects of the process and that the Task Force – as a group – completes the work within the structure and timeline outlined by *Boomer Volunteer Engagement: Collaborate Today, Thrive Tomorrow*. The book, together with this Tool Kit, is the map to help your non-profit reach its destination of Boomer Volunteer Engagement. The co-facilitators are the navigators and guides along the journey.

The co-facilitators' responsibility is to effectively involve all the Task Force members in the work at hand and ensure their continued forward progress. They lead the meetings, provide a structure for the Task Force to hold itself accountable, and ensure that they remain on track with the work and the timeline. The Task Force is responsible for generating the work, making their own decisions, ensuring organizational support and buy-in, and tracking their progress. Throughout the process, co-facilitators are there to support and guide, providing insights, suggestions, and all of the tools the Task Force will need along the way.

In order to be successful, the co-facilitators should:

- Become familiar with the organization, its mission, its current volunteer practices, its strategic plan, and more.
- Ensure a productive and positive tone in the meetings by establishing expectations and norms of behavior within the team and enthusiastically presenting the model of Boomer Volunteer Engagement and its benefits.
- Establish clear expectations and shared vision of the anticipated outcomes early on.
- Come prepared to each meeting – be familiar with the process, agenda, and expected next steps and outcomes.
- Hold the Task Force accountable for their commitments.

As the co-facilitators do their job, the Task Force is responsible for:

- Assessing the current needs of the organization.
- Becoming familiar with trends of Boomer volunteerism.
- Identifying and selecting a pilot project in which high-impact volunteers will be cultivated and used to build organizational capacity.
- Developing new, high-impact volunteer positions and cultivating individuals to successfully fill those positions.
- Monitoring progress and providing support to those implementing the pilot.
- Assessing the success of the pilot and evaluating it for sustainability into the future.
- Throughout, modeling the power and potential of staff and volunteer collaborations.

 TOOLS

- **Co-Facilitation Agreement Checklist**
- **Introductory Communication to Task Force**
- **Assessment of Organizational Volunteer Engagement**

- Ensure co-facilitators are prepared by reading the book *Boomer Volunteer Engagement* and becoming familiar with this Tool Kit.
- Hold preparation meetings between the co-facilitators to review materials and review the **Co-Facilitation Agreement Checklist**.
- Develop and distribute an **Introductory Communication to the Task Force** from the co-facilitators, in order to ensure that all Task Force members have appropriate expectations for the endeavor and prepare for their first meeting by completing the **Assessment of Organizational Volunteer Engagement**.

Co-Facilitation Agreement Checklist

WHAT: The following questions and checklist are designed to guide a conversation between the two co-facilitators and should be customized to the particular organization and to the personalities and strengths of the individuals involved.

WHY: When two individuals partner to co-facilitate a rich and complex process such as this volunteer engagement initiative, the process and everyone involved benefit from a frank conversation about how to divide and share the role of co-facilitators.

HOW: Use this checklist as a guide for a conversation and be sure to take notes and make explicit agreements about the chart of tasks. Tasks that should be equally shared are already checked for you. The rest is negotiable.

1. Strengths and Opportunities

What individual strengths does each of us bring to this process? What would each of us like to gain from this process?

2. Past Experience

Share some of our past experience in facilitation. What did we each enjoy? What were our challenges?

3. Concerns and Anticipation

What excited each of us about this initiative and this role? What concerns, if any, do we have about the initiative or about this partnership? How can we address them moving forward?

4. Dividing the Work

Use the following checklist to assign some of the major areas of responsibility as co-facilitators in order to share the workload and have clear agreements about each of our roles in the process.

Task	Co-Facilitator 1	Co-Facilitator 2
• Prepare by reading all materials.	✓	✓
• Prepare for each meeting.	✓	✓
• Distribute meeting agendas to Task Force prior to meeting.		
• Confirm room arrangement.		
• Take notes at the meetings.		
• Distribute notes to Task Force.		
• Follow up on deliverables from Task Force members.		
• Have a debrief conversation after each meeting.	✓	✓

Introductory Communication

WHAT: This is an outline of a communication to be developed by the co-facilitators and distributed to all of the Task Force members before their first Work Session.

WHY: The purpose of this communication is to establish a common understanding of the work to be undertaken, the timeline, and the expected preparation for the first Work Session.

HOW: Use this outline as a guide to develop your own introductory communication.

Dear Task Force Members,

Thank you for participating in the Boomer Volunteer Engagement Task Force for [our organization]. Our work over the next six months will be exciting and challenging and will help us to break new ground in the ways we engage volunteers to help fulfill our mission. We are writing to you as the co-facilitators for this process and we want to share with you how much we are looking forward to getting started.

Our first Task Force Work Session is scheduled for [insert date and time] and we will be meeting in [insert location]. This Work Session is scheduled for 2 hours, to ensure sufficient time to set the stage for the rest of our work. We will be scheduling our work so that we will generally have one meeting per month for six months. However, we will be meeting twice in our first month since we have much to discuss. During the first month's sessions, we will review the whole process, review trends in Boomer volunteerism, develop a case statement, and begin the process of selecting a pilot project designed to demonstrate the power and potential of high-impact volunteer engagement.

In order to make the most of our time together, we ask that you complete the following prior to our first Work Session:

- Read the Introduction and Chapters 1, 2, 3, and 5 of *Boomer Volunteer Engagement*.
- Complete the attached **Assessment of Organizational Volunteer Engagement**.
- Review the **Task Force Member Position Description**.

Please note that you should complete the assessment to the best of your knowledge, which means answering even the questions you may not feel you know enough to answer. Use your best judgment and experience to inform your answers. We have enclosed the Task Force Members Position Description as a reference to remind you of the role you have accepted and what you can expect from our work together.

We look forward to meeting with you on [insert date] and, in the meantime, please feel free to contact us with any questions. Thank you again for being part of this pioneering effort!

Respectfully,

[Insert names and contact information of the two co-facilitators]

Assessment of Organizational Volunteer Engagement

WHAT: This assessment is designed to help benchmark the organization's current volunteer engagement practices.

WHY: The results of this Assessment provide a snapshot of where the organization currently stands in terms of Boomer Volunteer Engagement and will help identify areas that would benefit from some strategic interventions in the form of a Boomer Volunteer Engagement pilot project.

HOW: Prior to the first Task Force work session, have all the Task Force members complete this assessment and bring their results to the first meeting for discussion. Co-facilitators should retain copies of the completed Assessments after the results are discussed at the first Task Force Work Session.

YOU . . .	Score 1 if you . . .	Score 2 if you . . .	Score 3 if you . . .
Organizational Support for Volunteers			
Involve volunteers in all aspects of organizational life.	Have staff and/or a few dedicated volunteers do most of the work.	Have a volunteer presence in all aspects of organizational activities and programming.	Mandate that staff and leadership utilize volunteers in their work.
Allocate resources, including budget, space, and tools, for volunteer engagement.	Assume that volunteers are "free" and do not require resources.	Have a budget for volunteer resources.	Reflect in your annual budget detailed expenses for volunteers, including supplies, space, software, training, recruitment, staff time, and recognition.
Train staff and board leadership to work effectively with volunteers.	Assume staff and key leadership know how to work with volunteers.	Reflect responsibility for volunteer engagement in staff and lay leadership position descriptions.	Provide formal training to staff and lay leadership on how to work with volunteers.
Needs Assessment and Program Planning			
Have defined why volunteers are a strategic priority for the organization.	Use volunteers for activities and programs as they are needed.	Have identified volunteers as leaders and helpers in moving the organization forward.	Have a written philosophy statement about volunteer engagement that identifies volunteers as an indispensable channel for ideas on organizational direction and operations, programs, and activities.
Include volunteer engagement in risk management planning.	Do not consider volunteer assignments in your risk assessment.	Evaluate all volunteer assignments for risk.	Have appropriate insurance for volunteer engagement and evaluate/update as necessary.

YOU . . .	Score 1 if you . . .	Score 2 if you . . .	Score 3 if you . . .
Effective Recruitment and Cultivation			
Have written position descriptions for all volunteer assignments.	Verbally explain to volunteers what they are going to do.	Have a position description for each volunteer assignment.	Conduct an annual (at minimum) review and update of all position descriptions.
Have a process for volunteer cultivation.	Do recruitment exclusively through announcements in the newsletter, website postings, etc.	Figure out who knows prospective volunteers and have them do the recruiting.	Have a written strategic recruitment plan for all volunteer assignments and needs.
Maintain current and accurate records on volunteers.	Do not track volunteer involvement.	Have a record of all volunteers and what they do for the organization.	Integrate volunteer records with membership and donor information.
Interviewing and Placement			
Design volunteer assignments for a wide range of skills, ages, and interests.	Rely on a specific group of volunteers (e.g., stay-at-home mothers, retired, etc.) to get the work done.	Include all age groups and demographics among your volunteers.	Design assignments specifically to reflect a wide range of skills and interests and not limit work to clerical and administrative positions.
Screen and place volunteers in assignments that are right for them and the organization.	Let anyone volunteer for anything.	Match volunteers to the assignment that aligns with their interests.	Recruit volunteers based on their preferences, the skills they willingly share, and the relevant qualifications for the job.
Orientation and Planning			
Have written policies and procedures for volunteer engagement.	Assume that volunteers know what is acceptable for them to do.	Have some policies that relate to volunteer involvement.	Have detailed written policies and procedures and orient all volunteers to these guidelines.

YOU . . .	Score 1 if you . . .	Score 2 if you . . .	Score 3 if you . . .
Supervision and Support			
Hold volunteers accountable for what they do.	Cannot fire a volunteer.	Clarify for volunteers the limits and boundaries of their assignments.	Have staff and leadership follow up with volunteers to make sure they accomplish what they set out to do, releasing them as needed.
Actively solicit volunteer input in decisions that affect them.	Have volunteers do whatever they are assigned.	Encourage current volunteers to give feedback.	Have a system in place for collecting and reflecting on volunteer feedback on decisions that affect them.
Strategies for Sustainability (Retention)			
Have volunteer assignments that are meaningful and that impact the ability of the organization to achieve its mission.	Design volunteer assignments around having people do the work of the staff and/ or board of directors.	Design volunteer assignments to have an impact on the mission of the organization.	Reflect a diversity of work in volunteer assignments, from direct service to program delivery, and incorporate high-level assignments, such as the provision of professional services.
Ensure that staff and leadership recognize volunteers informally and formally.	Host an annual recognition event for volunteers.	Give frequent recognition to volunteers from the board, staff, and other volunteer leaders.	Acknowledge the successes of volunteer endeavors in personalized ways through sharing celebratory information in collateral materials (e.g., the website, newsletters, announcements, emails, and written materials), through letters, and through customized networking opportunities with organizational leaders and others.

Key

Do you score mostly 3s? If so, you are well on your way to having an outstanding process for Boomer volunteer engagement. Your organization understands the benefits of a culture that embraces and celebrates volunteerism.

Do you score mostly 2s? Then your volunteer engagement process has room for improvement. Look at the number 3 answers to see where you have opportunities to improve your volunteer engagement practices.

Do you score mostly 1s? It is not unusual to start developing a volunteer engagement strategy from the ground up. Identify specific ways to develop greater competency in volunteer engagement and nurture volunteer talent.

Task Force Work Session 1

Planning for a Culture of Volunteer Engagement

KEY OUTCOMES

1. After this 2-part Work Session, Task Force members will have a broader understanding of Baby Boomers and their characteristics as they relate to volunteerism.

2. Task Force members will be able to distinguish between traditional volunteer management and collaborative volunteer engagement.

3. The Task Force will have systematically assessed the current volunteer engagement practices within the organization and identified strengths and opportunities.

4. The Task Force will have identified needs within the organization that can be addressed through high-impact Boomer Volunteer Engagement.

5. The Task Force will create a powerful case statement to use in marketing the work of the Task Force to the organization.

6. The Task Force will have begun developing a Work Plan for a project which will be used to demonstrate the power and potential of Boomer Volunteer Engagement.

NOTE: This month's efforts lay the foundation for the rest of the work ahead. The list of Key Outcomes is a hearty one for this first month. As such, we suggest breaking the first Work Session into two 2-hour meetings, and have included agendas for both. If you choose to launch the Task Force with a half-day retreat, we encourage you to do so and adapt the agendas accordingly. Regardless of how you schedule the two parts of the Work Session, remember that investing sufficient time up front on the activities and conversations suggested here will save time and make the process more efficient and successful over the long run.

Related Material in *Boomer Volunteer Engagement*:

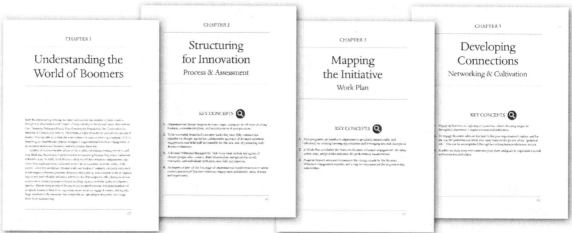

[THE FRAMEWORK]

As described in *Boomer Volunteer Engagement*, successful and sustainable organizational change starts small and it grows by building on the success of those small steps taken at the start. In other words, it is important to start with a few discrete innovations. By evaluating those innovations, tweaking them where necessary, and then adapting or replicating the elements that work, momentum builds and eventually brings about a larger, enterprise-wide change. The biggest challenge is in selecting the right innovation to make at the beginning. Selecting the right pilot project is critical. The goal is to pick a pilot project that is likely to succeed. Resist the temptation to start with areas that are

3

the most challenging. Instead, select a pilot project that fulfills a strategic need, that takes advantage of individuals who are already excited by the idea of high-impact volunteer engagement, and that, simply put, will make a compelling story in the end. The goal of the pilot project is to succeed and, in its success, to inspire others to jump on board and engage high impact volunteers in their work areas as well.

With this goal of inspiring others in mind, the Task Force will start thinking about the messages they want to communicate to the rest of the organization. To assist in this process, the **Case Statement** exercise will help the group to focus on key messages. These powerful messages help to create a tipping point within the organization to get leadership, staff, and volunteers to think differently about volunteerism and the organization's commitment to it as a core strategy for capacity building.

Next, the Task Force focuses on the selection of the pilot project. This selection process begins with the **Needs Assessment** which is designed to identify existing organizational needs that could be addressed through strategic volunteer engagement. To help select from the list of needs, a new tool is included. The **Pilot Project Selection Questions** are a filter through which the Task Force can discuss the list of possible projects. Using the Selection Questions to guide the discussion, the Task Force should be able to make a decision about which pilot project to select and implement. In the meantime, keep the list of other pilot ideas because their time may come! Remember, the goal is for this pilot to be the first of many discrete innovations that, together, result in a larger culture shift organizationally, a shift that brings the organization closer to enacting a dynamic culture of high level volunteer engagement.

Finally, the **Work Plan** is designed to create a plan that will get results. By thinking about vision, impact, and outcome, the Work Plan will help to propel the group into its preferred future. The Work Plan creates the opportunity to think intentionally and strategically about resources, actions, and yield needed to support organizational change.

 TOOLS

- Assessment of Organizational Volunteer Engagement (completed as preparation for this Work Session)
- Agenda for Task Force Work Session 1 (part A)
- Needs Assessment
- Case Statement
- Agenda for Task Force Work Session 1 (part B)
- Pilot Project Selection Questions
- Work Plan
- Co-Facilitator Work Session Report

 MAKING IT HAPPEN

- Launch the Task Force by holding the initial Work Session, in two parts (or, as noted above, in a half-day retreat of at least 4 hours).
- Work Session 1, Part A focuses on the foundation of Boomer Volunteer Engagement and developing a case statement to be used in communicating with the rest of the organization. During this session, the Task Force will complete these exercises:
  – **Review results of the Assessment of Organizational Volunteer Engagement**
  – **Needs Assessment**
  – **Case Statement**
- Part B of the Work Session begins the process of identifying a pilot project and includes these exercises:
  – **Pilot Project Selection Questions**
  – **Work Plan**
- At the conclusion of the work session, the co-facilitators should work together to complete:
  – **Co-Facilitator Work Session Report**

Agenda for Task Force Work Session 1 (Part A)
Making the Case for Volunteer Engagement

WHAT: This is an agenda for Part A of the first Task Force Work Session. (We suggest breaking the first Work Session into two 2-hour meetings, and have included agendas for both. If you choose to launch the Task Force with a half-day retreat, we encourage you to do so and adapt the agendas accordingly.)

WHY: The purpose of this meeting is to review the foundation of Boomer volunteer engagement and to develop a case statement for volunteer engagement.

HOW: Use this agenda to plan and guide the Task Force Work Session.

Making the Case for Volunteer Engagement

Participants
Co-facilitators
Task Force Members

Meeting Length
2 hours

Prep Work
The Task Force members will have read the Introduction and Chapters 1, 2, 3, and 5 of the book, ***Boomer Volunteer Engagement***, and completed the **Assessment of Organizational Volunteer Engagement**.

 DISCUSSION GUIDE

I. Setting the Stage – Reviewing the Process, Roles, and Expectations

Task Force Roles
- Review the **Task Force Process and Timeline.**
- Assure clear understanding of the **Organizational and Task Force Commitments and Expectations.**
- For each of you, as members of this Task Force, what do you hope to get out of this process? What is your stake in this volunteer engagement initiative?

Organizational Goals
- What do you think our organizational leadership hopes to get out of this project?
- Have you reviewed the **Organizational Roles and Expectations** and the **Task Force Position Description**? Do you have any questions?

3

II. Overview of Boomer Volunteer Engagement

Current Organizational Practice
- Have the Task Force members share their results, reactions, and thoughts about the scoring on the Assessment of Organizational Volunteer Engagement.
- From our reading thus far, what have we learned about the potential that engaging skilled Boomer volunteers holds for our organization? How can it change our future? What did we find surprising or eye-opening?

Boomer Characteristics
- What shifts have you observed in our organization in the past few years in terms of volunteerism?
- What have you learned both from personal experience and from the book, *Boomer Volunteer Engagement*, about the Boomer generation and what Boomers seek from their volunteer experiences?

Foundation of Boomer Volunteer Engagement
- Boomer Volunteer Engagement is inherently collaborative, strategic, skills-based, and impactful. As a result, it builds organizational capacity and builds community. How does this resonate with our organization currently? What possibilities can we begin to see in light of this perspective?

Paradigm Shift
- This work requires a new language descriptive of engagement instead of management. After reading about this in the book, how would such a shift affect your role as staff and as volunteers in each of these areas, namely cultivation, negotiation, support, performance measurement, acknowledgment, and sustainability?

III. Assessing Needs

As we have discussed, Boomer Volunteer Engagement is a strategy that can help the organization fulfill critical needs and build capacity for the future. A good place to start our journey is to assess the organization's current needs.

Needs Assessment ✿✿

- Distribute the **Needs Assessment** and ask participants to complete questions 1-5 individually. Give the group a chance to share answers and discuss as a group. Compile a list of the needs identified by the group.

IV. Making the Case

As with any important organizational endeavor, having a clear and compelling case statement clarifies the rationale, communicates the ultimate vision for success, and provides clear and consistent messages. In what other situations does our organization use case statements? What has made those case statements effective (or not)?

Case Statement ✿✿

- Distribute the **Case Statement** template. Discuss as a group to identify the key messages about the shift from a culture of volunteer management to a culture of volunteer engagement. Fill out the Case Statement template as a group.

Next Steps

Before leaving Part A of this Work Session, be sure to schedule your next 2-3 Work Sessions as a group. Each of those sessions should be scheduled for 2 hours.

Between now and the next session, the Task Force members should:

- Review the Case Statement drafted today.
- Review the materials covered in the chapters in *Boomer Volunteer Engagement* already read, especially Chapter 3 on developing a Work Plan.

Needs Assessment

WHAT: This is an assessment tool to help Task Force members reflect on not only what work is currently being done at the organization, but also what could be done if more resources were available.

WHY: It is helpful for Task Force members to see what is possible when volunteers are engaged in building the organization's capacity to address the dreams and challenges it faces.

HOW: Use this Needs Assessment after ensuring that the Task Force is familiar with the current state of the organization and its volunteer engagement practices. Have individuals complete this assessment individually then discuss as a group.

1. What are the dreams for our
   organization that require more
   people, expertise, money, or tools
   to accomplish?

2. What are the problems and challenges
   that our organization is currently
   experiencing?

3. What is our organization currently
   doing that we would like to increase,
   replicate, or expand?

3

4. What is an area of your division/
   department that is always underutilized
   or understaffed, or seems constantly
   overloaded?

5. What specific skills and resources
   would our organization's personnel
   need to fulfill your dreams? To meet
   its challenges?

6. Who in our circles of influence
   embraces volunteers and would be
   open to building the organization's
   capacity to address these dreams and
   challenges?

7. Who are our Mavens? Who are the
   experts on volunteering? Who are the
   experts on projects our organization
   wants to begin or complete?

_____

_____

_____

_____

_____

_____

_____

_____

8. Who are our Connectors? Who seems
   connected to everyone in particular
   communities we want to tap? (Which
   communities?)

_____

_____

_____

_____

_____

_____

_____

_____

9. Who are our Salespeople? Who can sell
   someone the shirt off her back and
   make her glad to buy it?

_____

_____

_____

_____

_____

_____

_____

_____

3

10. Are you an answer to any of the previous three questions? (Which ones? Why?)

11. With what could our organization utilize a consultant or specialist to help you—now and in the future—work toward vision and mission fulfillment?

12. What areas of our organization would benefit from program outcome evaluation?

Based on these Needs Assessment data, what are three entrepreneurial volunteer assignments or volunteer leadership positions that would be an asset to our organization?

1. _____
   _____
   _____
   _____
   _____

2. _____
   _____
   _____
   _____
   _____

3. _____
   _____
   _____
   _____
   _____

3

Case Statement

What: This is a template for the Case Statement that will create key messages to the organization.

Why: A Case Statement is important for creating understanding of and support for the volunteer engagement initiative.

How: Refer to Chapter 5 in *Boomer Volunteer Engagement* for detailed instructions on how to create a case statement.

Case Statement

Element	Our Case Statement
Background on how initiative began and why it is a strategic priority	
Connection to organizational mission and vision	
Financial supporters, including stakeholders and powerful allies	
Examples of success stories and exemplary programs and services	

Element	Our Case Statement
Speaking Points	
Elevator Speech	

Agenda for Task Force Work Session 1 (Part B)
Selecting a Pilot Project

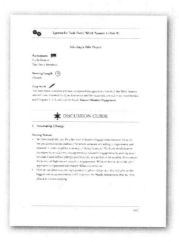

WHAT: This is an agenda for the Part B of Task Force Work Session 1. (We suggest breaking the first Work Session into two 2-hour meetings, and have included agendas for both. If you choose to launch the Task Force with a half-day retreat, we encourage you to do so and adapt the agendas accordingly.)

WHY: The purpose of this meeting is to select a pilot project and develop a Work Plan for it.

HOW: Use this agenda to plan and guide the Task Force Work Session.

Selecting a Pilot Project

Participants
Co-facilitators
Task Force Members

Meeting Length
2 hours

Prep Work
The Task Force members will have completed the agenda for Part A of this Work Session and will have reviewed the Case Statement and the materials covered in the Introduction and Chapters 1, 2, 3, and 5 of the book, *Boomer Volunteer Engagement*.

⚙ DISCUSSION GUIDE

I. Innovating Change

Getting Started
- We have made the case for a Boomer Volunteer Engagement Initiative. How do we get started on this endeavor? In which areas are we willing to experiment and innovate in order to pilot a new way of doing business? The book details how to transition from volunteer management to volunteer engagement by starting small through a well-defined pilot project that can, in a period of six months, demonstrate the power of high-impact volunteer engagement. What excites us about the pilot approach to organizational change? What concerns us?
- How do we determine the right project to pilot – the project that will give us the biggest return on investment? Let's return to the **Needs Assessment** that we completed at our last meeting.

Needs Assessment ✿✿

- What were the needs that we identified last time? As a group, rank those needs into high priority and low priority groupings, then keep that list visible as we move on to the process of selecting a pilot.

Pilot Project Selection Questions ✿✿

- Discuss which project would be the most logical to select for a small pilot utilizing Boomer Volunteer Engagement as a strategy. Cull the list down to the top two or three possibilities. Distribute the Pilot Project Selection Questions exercise and, as a group, complete the questions for each of the pilot projects under discussion. Use the exercise to guide group discussion.
- Once all the possible projects are reviewed in light of the Pilot Selection Questions, we have the information we need to make a decision about which one to develop. The Task Force is now ready to vote and finalize the decision about which project to pilot first.
  - For each possibility under consideration, give a "thumbs up" (endorsement), "thumb sideways" (not sure), or "thumbs down" (rejection) for the idea.
  - We will select the idea that receives the most "thumbs up" votes.

II. Planning for Success

- What forms of Work Plans (or logic models) have you used before? How have they helped to guide your work and achieve intended results?
- A Work Plan is essential to any change initiative. The Work Plan establishes the vision and impact, outlines key action steps, and provides indicators against which leaders can measure progress.

Work Plan ✿✿

Distribute copies of the Work Plan definitions sheet and the blank Work Plan.

- Review the elements of the Work Plan detailed on page 49 of *Boomer Volunteer Engagement*. How does the "Vision" section relate to the "Sustained Outcome" section?
- As a group, complete the Work Plan for the selected pilot project. We will likely have time to only complete a portion of the Work Plan at this meeting. We will start with the Vision and the Initial Impact and Sustained Outcomes sections to demonstrate

3

how those columns should relate closely to each other. (See Chapter 3, Mapping the Initiative, for background on this concept.)

- Before completing the work for the day, identify which Task Force member(s) will be completing the draft and distributing it for review and comments from the rest of the group before the next Work Session.

III. Next Steps

Before leaving this Work Session, be sure to schedule your next two or three Work Sessions. Each of the Work Sessions should be 2 hours in length.

Between now and the next session, the Task Force members should:
- Read Chapters 4, 5, and 6 of *Boomer Volunteer Engagement.*
- Complete a draft of the project Work Plan.

Pilot Project Selection Questions

WHAT: This is a discussion tool to use to help select the focus of the pilot program.

WHY: Selecting the right pilot project is key to the success of the volunteer engagement initiative in general. Ensuring that you have a project that is leveraged for success will position the Task Force, the new volunteers, and, ultimately, the whole organization for a meaningful and impactful volunteer engagement initiative.

HOW: Review the list of possible projects and, after considering them in light of the Pilot Project Selection Questions, discuss which project will be selected.

Pilot Project Selection Questions

For each possible pilot project, consider these questions and use the answers to determine whether this is the best way to intervene with strategic volunteer engagement.

Potential Pilot Project _____

Does it play to a strength? _____

Will it come as a surprise to any key stakeholders? _____

What changes to current practice are needed? _____

_____

_____

_____

Do existing volunteers and staff have the expertise and time to carry this out – or need to be trained?

_____

Are more or different people needed? _____

Are new position descriptions needed? _____

What are the biggest anticipated challenges? _____

_____

_____

_____

What are you willing to invest? _____

_____

_____

What aren't you willing to invest? _____

_____

_____

_____

Is it sustainable? _____

Work Plan

WHAT: This is a template for the Work Plan that will outline the scope of the project and be the common reference for the Task Force to track progress.

WHY: A Work Plan establishes the vision and impact of the project, outlines key action steps, and provides indicators against which leaders can measure progress.

HOW: Refer to Chapter 3 in *Boomer Volunteer Engagement* for detailed instructions on how to complete a Work Plan and to see sample Work Plans. The Task Force should begin to fill in this Work Plan template for the project that will likely be the pilot project. The Task Force, or selected members from the team, will be responsible for completing the draft between Work Session 1 and Work Session 2.

⚙✿ Work Plan

Vision Statement	Resources	Action	Yield	Initial Impact	Sustained Outcome

Co-Facilitator Work Session Report

WHAT: This is an assessment tool for the co-facilitators to use following each Task Force Work Session to reflect on their facilitation and to track their own progress as facilitators.

WHY: Taking time to reflect on these questions following each Work Session will ensure that the co-facilitators stay in tune with each other, identify successful facilitation tactics, and strategize ways to improve where needed. This process can also help to keep stakeholders informed of progress and needs for additional support. By sharing this information, it can build support and help cultivate champions for the effort within the organization.

HOW: Following the Work Session, the two co-facilitators should sit down to complete this form jointly and discuss the answers openly and honestly. This can also be shared with organizational leaders (the executive, the Board, or others who are tracking progress on this initiative and providing support).

Co-Facilitator Work Session Report

Use this form to record the results of your meetings with the Task Force.

Co-Facilitators _____

Organization _____

Meeting Date _____ Time _____

Attended by _____

Did we complete the agenda? (If no, what sections were not covered and why?) _____

_____

_____

What issues or questions were raised? _____

_____

_____

What were the successes of this meeting? _____

_____

_____

What were the challenges? _____

_____

_____

What are our next steps? _____

_____

_____

How can we work together to keep the endeavor moving forward? Do we need any additional support? If so, what is our plan to request that support?

_____

_____

_____

_____

Task Force Work Session 2

Creating Opportunities

KEY OUTCOMES

As a result of this Work Session, participants will:

1. Confirm selection of the project to demonstrate the power and potential of Boomer Volunteer Engagement.

2. Finalize development of the project Work Plan.

3. Identify two or three high-impact volunteer opportunities and begin developing position descriptions for each of them.

4. Develop a strategic message for marketing those positions and begin broadcasting that message.

5. Begin to track progress against the Work Plan.

Related Material in *Boomer Volunteer Engagement*:

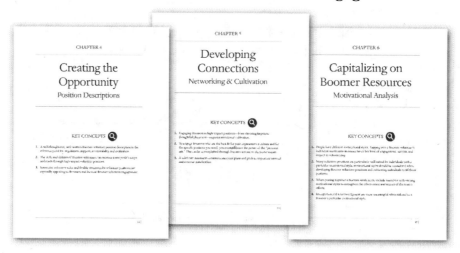

[THE FRAMEWORK]

Once the focus of the pilot project has been determined, the next exciting challenge is to develop volunteer positions that will serve to advance the pilot project's goals and successfully attract individuals with the skills and interest to collaborate with staff and/ or lead the initiative. In order to develop positions that take the organization's volunteer engagement in new directions, it's important to think in new ways. How could a local architect, graphic designer, writer, editor, carpenter, event planner, or business consultant, for example, engage with you for a discrete period and measurably help you achieve the goals of the pilot project while also gaining personal benefit or exposure for his/her business? If the Task Force is having difficulty brainstorming this issue, then simply ask, "Imagine that we received a small grant to hire a skilled professional to help in some small way over the next three months and we found the perfect person to hire, who would that be and what would we want the outcome to be?" That should help move the conversation beyond traditional volunteer roles and open up possibilities of truly high-impact volunteer positions.

When developing high-impact volunteer positions, be sure to design them so that they achieve the larger goals of a volunteer engagement initiative. Are the positions structured so that they meet the desires of Boomers and the generations that follow?

4

Are they inherently flexible? Results-focused? Skills-based? By doing so, will they attract a different type of volunteer? Is this position structured to allow this volunteer to build organizational capacity beyond what staff alone can accomplish? In other words, does the position help to change the paradigm? In order for the pilot endeavor to succeed as both an isolated project and as the start of a larger shift throughout the organization, it is important that the volunteer positions align with the strategic goals of the pilot, that they represent an authentic collaboration with staff and/or other volunteers, and that they model the change you want to see in the organization over time.

 TOOLS

- Agenda for Task Force Work Session 2
- Volunteer Position Description
- Strategic Messages
- Task Force Progress Report
- Co-Facilitator Work Session Report

✅ MAKING IT HAPPEN

- Finalize project selection and Work Plan draft.
- Hold second Task Force Work Session, focusing on creating volunteer opportunities. Exercises include:
  - **Volunteer Position Description**
  - **Strategic Messages**
- At the conclusion of the Work Session, both the Task Force and the co-facilitators should track their progress using the appropriate tracking tools:
  - **Task Force Progress Report**
  - **Co-Facilitator Work Session Report**

Agenda for Task Force Work Session 2
Creating Opportunities

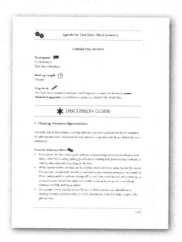

WHAT: This is an agenda for the second work session of the Task Force. Work Session 2 should be scheduled to last at least 2 hours.

WHY: The purpose of this meeting is to confirm the selected pilot project, to finalize the Work Plan, to develop high-impact volunteer opportunities, and design strategic messages for those volunteer opportunities.

HOW: Use this agenda to plan and guide the Task Force Work Session.

Creating Opportunities

Participants

Co-facilitators

Task Force Members

Meeting Length

2 hours

Prep Work

The Task Force members will have read Chapters 4, 5, and 6 of the book, *Boomer Volunteer Engagement*, and will have completed a draft of the Work Plan.

 DISCUSSION GUIDE

I. Creating Volunteer Opportunities

The next step in this endeavor is to identify the volunteer positions needed to complete the pilot project and to structure these positions in ways that will attract skilled Boomer volunteers.

Exercise: Volunteer Roles

- In the book, we have read a great deal about structuring volunteer positions in new ways, either by retooling existing positions or creating new positions that embody an entirely new approach to getting work done.

- What opportunities exist that can be restructured to be more attractive for Boomers? For example, certain staff members may need some research assistance. Are some of those tasks possible to achieve during off hours? How could shared online workspace or access to the intranet be utilized to enable a stay-at-home parent or working volunteer to help with those tasks?

- As a group, review and discuss the Volunteer Roles exercise and identify some existing volunteer positions that could be retooled or created to help complete the pilot project.

II. Position Descriptions

Ask the group to generate a list of two or three high-impact volunteer positions that they might develop, based on the results of their Needs Assessment (completed at the first Work Session) and the pilot project they have selected.

Exercise: Creating Position Descriptions ⚙⚙
Distribute the Position Description template and ask the group to break into smaller groups of two or three individuals. Each group should draft a Position Description Title and Key Responsibilities for a position that would be essential to successful implementation of the pilot project. If time allows, also ask them to draft the Initial Impact and Sustained Outcomes of the position. Share their work as a group.

III. Networking and Cultivation

Once we have the position description developed, it is important to be strategic about how and to whom we will spread the word about that opportunity and ensure that the message reaches qualified potential volunteers.

- How does our organization currently reach potential volunteers? Newsletters? Website? Online volunteer matching engines? Mailings? Targeted personal asks? Online social networking? How else?
- It is important to think about the target audience when developing a plan to market a new volunteer opportunity. For each new position description, discuss these questions:
  – Who would want to do this assignment and why?
  – Where would we find such individuals? Are they already in our circle of influence (donors, clients and their families, existing volunteers, vendors)? Where?
  – Who is the best person to make the "ask?"
  – What will they need to know to be successful?
  – Who among our current stakeholders might be the answer to some of the previous questions?

4

IV. Strategic Messaging

A message is a useful, concise invitation to learn more about the position description. In Chapter 5 of the book, *Boomer Volunteer Engagement*, there is a template to help develop a message that could be used on an online volunteer matching search engine, used as a script for a phone call, posted on Facebook or other Boomer-friendly sites, and in many other ways.

Exercise: Strategic Messages ✿✿
As you design the recruitment message, be sure to address these considerations:
- Communicate how the volunteer's work will impact the organization.
- Highlight the needs the volunteer's effort is designed to address.
- Tell the potential volunteer why you think he/she is well suited for the job.

Distribute the Messages template and ask the group to draft a strategic message for one of the position descriptions they began developing earlier (if it is a large group, break into small work groups and report out). Encourage them to consider:
- What is the job?
- How will the volunteer help?
- Who would want to do this job?
- Where will you find the right volunteers?
- How can they personalize the invitation?

Discuss as a group.

V. Progress Report

Distribute the Progress Report template and lead a brief discussion about the importance of completing a Progress Report between Work Sessions and submitting the copy to the co-facilitators one week prior to the next Work Session. A Progress Report is a way for the Task Force to systematically track accomplishments, avoid being surprised by progress or problems, and intervene early when needed. In addition, Progress Reports track accomplishments and provide information to use in reports to organizational leaders and stakeholders.

- Who from the Task Force will be responsible for completing the Progress Reports and getting comments from the rest of team before submitting to the co-facilitators?
- Is there anyone else who should see copies of the Progress Reports (for example, Board members, the CEO, others)?

VI. Next Steps

Remind the Task Force of the time and location of the next meeting and ask them to do the following in preparation for that meeting:

- Read Chapters 7, 8, and 9 of **Boomer Volunteer Engagement**.
- Complete the Position Description for their volunteer positions.
- Complete the Messaging template for those positions and begin to market those messages through strategically selected media.

Volunteer Position Description

WHAT: A Position Description details the responsibilities and expectations of the volunteer assignment and is the basis for cultivation, selection, and support of the volunteer.

WHY: A carefully considered, well-written volunteer position description is the reference point for negotiation, support, accountability, and evaluation. Therefore it is key to the success of any staff/volunteer collaboration.

HOW: Use this Position Description template as the guide to developing a new high-impact volunteer position to demonstrate the power and potential of such a role. The Position Description is a point of reference for negotiation and support between staff and volunteers. Chapter 4 of *Boomer Volunteer Engagement* details the elements of a well-written position description.

Position Overview

_____

_____

_____

_____

Title: _____

_____

Key responsibilities: _____

_____

_____

_____

Initial impact: _____

_____

_____

_____

Sustained outcomes: _____

_____

_____

_____

Training: _____

_____

_____

_____

Support: _____

_____

_____

_____

Commitment: _____

_____

_____

Length of time: _____

_____

Amount of time: _____

_____

Specify evenings, weekdays, weekends: _____

_____

Location of volunteer assignment: _____

_____

_____

Qualifications: _____

_____

Skills: _____

_____

_____

Benefits: _____

_____

_____

_____

Strategic Messages

WHAT: This is a template to use when developing strategic messages designed to attract skilled individuals into high-impact volunteer positions.

WHY: The messages and communications methods that bring Boomers and the generations that follow into volunteering are different than those that successfully attracted previous generations. To attract skilled individuals into positions of leadership and/or collaboration, the messages must be well-crafted and should clearly highlight the impact of the position.

HOW: Refer to Chapter 5 of **Boomer Volunteer Engagement** for a detailed overview of strategic messaging and for tips on how to write messages and where to broadcast them.

4

Title:

Call-to-Action:

Position Overview:

Task Force Progress Report

WHAT: This is a tracking tool for the Task Force members to use following each Task Force Work Session to reflect on their progress in implementing their Work Plan.

WHY: Benchmarking progress is important to ensure continued forward movement as well as to identify roadblocks and strategize effective ways to move beyond them. Progress Reports prevent unexpected surprises from derailing the entire initiative by alerting team members early on and enabling them to be nimble and flexible in finding ways to achieve the intended results. They help inform the co-facilitators of emerging issues so the Work Sessions can be tailored to address them. Progress Reports also help to keep stakeholders informed of progress and needs for additional support. By sharing this information, it can build support and help cultivate champions for the effort within the organization.

HOW: Refer to Chapter 3 in *Boomer Volunteer Engagement* for instructions on how to complete a Progress Report. Following the Work Session, members of the Task Force should work together to complete this form and submit it to the co-facilitators prior to the next Work Session. This can also be shared with organizational leaders (the executive, the Board, or others who are tracking progress on this initiative and providing support).

4

PROGRESS REPORT

Vision: _____

Element	Description	Indicators and Tools	Progress, Challenges, and Needs
Resources			
Action			
Yield			
Initial Impact			
Sustained Outcome			

Co-Facilitator Work Session Report

WHAT: This is an assessment tool for the co-facilitators to use following each Task Force Work Session to reflect on their facilitation and to track their own progress as facilitators.

WHY: Taking time to reflect on these questions following each Work Session will ensure that the co-facilitators stay in tune with each other, identify successful facilitation tactics, and strategize ways to improve where needed. This process can also help to keep stakeholders informed of progress and needs for additional support. By sharing this information, it can build support and help cultivate champions for the effort within the organization.

HOW: Following the Work Session, the two co-facilitators should sit down to complete this form jointly and discuss the answers openly and honestly. This can also be shared with organizational leaders (the executive, the Board, or others who are tracking progress on this initiative and providing support).

Co-Facilitator Work Session Report

Use this form to record the results of your meetings with the Task Force.

Co-facilitators _____

Organization _____

Meeting Date _____ Time _____

Attended by _____

Did we complete the agenda? (If no, what sections were not covered and why?) _____

_____

_____

What issues or questions were raised? _____

_____

_____

What were the successes of this meeting? _____

_____

_____

What were the challenges? _____

_____

_____

What are our next steps? _____

_____

_____

How can we work together to keep the endeavor moving forward? Do we need any additional support? If so, what is our plan to request that support?

_____

_____

_____

_____

Task Force Work Session 3

Interviewing, Negotiation, and Support

KEY OUTCOMES

As a result of this Work Session, participants will:

1. Learn effective interviewing techniques.

2. Have developed a series of interview questions to be used with candidates for their high-impact volunteer positions.

3. Be able to effectively support volunteers as partners and collaborators, rather than simply supervise them.

4. Be prepared to implement the pilot project of Boomer Volunteer Engagement.

Related Material in *Boomer Volunteer Engagement*:

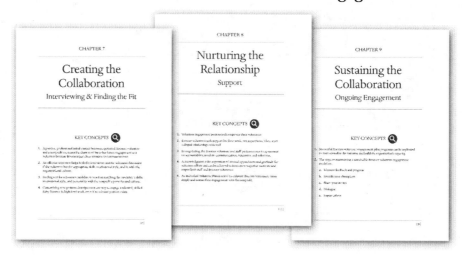

[THE FRAMEWORK]

Choosing the right volunteer for a position that is at the heart of this pilot project means knowing more than the candidates' basic skills and experience; choosing the right volunteer leader means learning about the candidates' adaptability and ways of thinking – and learning those things without adding hours to the interview and selection process.

In a world in which organizations are increasingly required to be nimble, creative, and entrepreneurial in management and program delivery, we must engage volunteer leaders who bring those traits to our table and who can partner with us in our efforts towards mission fulfillment. To identify which potential volunteers are nimble, creative, and entrepreneurial themselves, use a behaviorally-based interviewing style. The process can be boiled down to three steps that comprise a standard 30 or 60 minute interview: Tell it. Show it. Tweak it.[1]

1.   **Tell it**. Ask candidates to describe a situation in which they used the skills you are seeking in this position. For example, if the position is one leading a new pilot program,

---

1 Jennifer Rackow, "Tell It. Show It. Tweak It. Interviewing for 21st Century Volunteer Leaders," November 20, 2009, http://jffixler. com/tell-it-show-it-tweak-it-interviewing-21st-century-volunteer-leaders, (accessed March 16, 2010).

ask, "Please share an example of when you tried something and it failed. How did you handle it?"

2. Show it. Next, present the candidates with the opportunity to demonstrate some of those skills right there in the interview. For the potential pilot program leaders, ask the candidates to develop and share the first five steps they would take in developing the program concept, for example.

3. Tweak it. After the candidates have shared examples from the past and demonstrated their ability to think on their feet, problem-solve, and communicate their solutions, go a little deeper. Change the scenario you just presented and ask them to adapt. In other words, for potential pilot leaders, explain, "The funder of this pilot program has asked that, before we begin the program, we test its feasibility. How would you adapt your plan to incorporate feasibility testing?"

The three steps above add the chance to observe the candidates' approach to problem solving, understanding of your organization, communication style, ability to deal with stress, and more. Do they seek out additional information? Make decisions unilaterally or include collaboration in their plans? Shy away from sharing their views, present their opinions with confidence, or try to impress with their knowledge or connections? In other words, these steps – especially the third, in which they tweak their answer in response to real-world change scenarios – will reveal whether the candidate possesses the traits that are critical to being a successful partner with your nonprofit. The nimble, creative, entrepreneurial leaders will stand out.

⚙⚙ TOOLS

- Agenda for Task Force Work Session 3
- Interview Questions
- Task Force Progress Report
- Co-Facilitator Work Session Report

- Finalize the **Volunteer Position Description** and **Strategic Messages**.
- Hold the third Task Force Work Session, focusing on how to find the right fit for volunteer positions and how to effectively support those individuals once they are in the positions. Exercises include:
  – **Interview Questions**
- At the conclusion of the Work Session, both the Task Force and the co-facilitators should track their progress using the appropriate tracking tools:
  – **Task Force Progress Report**
  – **Co-Facilitator Work Session Report**

Agenda for Work Session 3
Interviewing, Negotiation, and Support

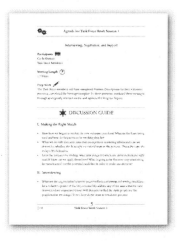

WHAT: This is an agenda for the third Work Session of the Task Force. Work Session 3 should be scheduled to last at least 90 minutes.

WHY: The purpose of this meeting is to be able to effectively interview individuals and determine if they are the right fit for the position, to strategize ways to provide support to high-impact volunteers, and to launch the pilot project following this Work Session.

HOW: Use this agenda to plan and guide the Task Force Work Session.

Interviewing, Negotiation, and Support

Participants
Co-facilitators
Task Force Members

Meeting Length
1.5 hours

Prep Work
The Task Force members will have completed Position Descriptions for their volunteer positions, completed the Messages template for those positions, marketed those messages through strategically selected media, and updated the Progress Report.

DISCUSSION GUIDE

I. Making the Right Match

- How have we begun to market the new volunteer positions? What methods are being used and how do they seem to be working thus far?
- What we do with the candidates that emerge from marketing efforts and how we determine whether the fit is right are critical steps in this process. This is the topic for today's Work Session.
- From the preparation reading, what new things did you learn about making the right match? How can we apply them here? What is going to be the most important thing for us to learn about the potential candidate in order to make our decision?

II. Interviewing

- What are the organization's current practices for interviewing and vetting candidates for a volunteer position? Do they successfully address any of the issues that we have determined are important? How? Will this process find the right people for the positions that we design? If not, how do we want to tweak the process?

5

- During an interview, what are the candidate's goals for the interview process? What are the organization's goals? How can we strategically structure an interview to successfully meet both sets of goals?

Exercise: Interview Questions ⚙⚙

Distribute the Interview Questions template and ask the group to brainstorm some questions for one of the positions they are currently trying to fill through this project. Either break into small groups and then reconvene to share and discuss or brainstorm as a group. After group discussion, decide on an interview strategy and who will conduct the interviews. If you have a volunteer engagement professional on staff, that individual may do the initial screening and then another Task Force member would do a secondary interview of top candidates.

III. Making the Offer

- Not everyone is the right fit for a skilled volunteer position. In fact, most people are not the right fit. So, what will we do when the fit is not there? What other positions are currently available in our organization? Can we create a list of other assignments that could be recommended to candidates who are not a good fit for this pilot position, but who might do well elsewhere in the institution?
- If it is a good fit, what steps do we take to make the offer? What is the value of refraining from making an offer at the end of an interview? Why wait until a few days or weeks following the interview?
- How do the recommendations in Chapter 7 of the book *Boomer Volunteer Engagement* compare to our current interview and placement practices?

IV. Negotiation

- What are the goals of the first meeting between staff and volunteer partners? As a Task Force, discuss what it really means to define the position in terms of results, to determine the level of authority for the position, and to hold each other accountable.
- How can the volunteer and staff member define what success will look like?

V. Support and Acknowledgment

- What does it really mean to be a true "supporter" of volunteer partners rather than a traditional "supervisor" of volunteers? Decide who will provide support and resources to the volunteer.
- How do we currently acknowledge or recognize our volunteers?
- What are some more personalized acknowledgments you think our volunteers would appreciate?
- What are some of the ways we could shift our culture from one of supervising volunteers to one of supporting them? How can we create an environment in which staff and volunteers provide some mutual acknowledgment?

VI. Checking Progress

- The last few steps in establishing an effective, collaborative relationship is to develop a system for checking progress on the mutually agreed upon outcomes of the work. What issues should the volunteer and staff explicitly address in regard to checking in and tracking progress?
- Here are a few questions to consider discussing during those regularly scheduled meetings:
  - How would you evaluate your progress?
  - Are you on target?
  - If not, what can we learn from this setback to be stronger in the future?
  - What has gone well and why?
  - What are some better ways of doing what we do?
  - How can we apply this information to help move the project forward?
  - Other?

VII. Next Steps

The Task Force now has all the tools it needs to begin implementing the pilot project. Remind the Task Force of the time and location of the next meeting and ask them to do the following in preparation for that meeting:

- Interview candidates and offer the position to those who best fit the positions.
- Negotiate the results of the work.
- Launch the pilot.
- Throughout, remember to track progress.
- Update the Progress Report and submit it to the co-facilitators one week prior to the next meeting. The Progress Report should include an update on progress, challenges, and adjustments to the plan.

Interview Questions

WHAT: This is a template to help develop effective questions to use during interviews with candidates for the new volunteer positions.

WHY: An effective interview helps both the interviewer and the potential volunteer determine whether the individual has the appropriate skills, motivational style, and fit with the organizational culture.

HOW: Use the definitions and suggestions in Chapter 7 of *Boomer Volunteer Engagement* as a guide to develop questions that can be used in an interview to ensure that interviewers get the information they seek with all candidates.

1. **Problem-Solving Question**

2. **Situational Question**

3. **Experiential Question**

4. **Skills Question**

Task Force Progress Report

WHAT: This is a tracking tool for the Task Force members to use following each Task Force Work Session to reflect on their progress in implementing their Work Plan.

WHY: Benchmarking progress is important to ensure continued forward movement as well as to identify roadblocks and strategize effective ways to move beyond them. Progress Reports prevent unexpected surprises from derailing the entire initiative by alerting team members early on and enabling them to be nimble and flexible in finding ways to achieve the intended results. They help inform the co-facilitators of emerging issues so the Work Sessions can be tailored to address them. Progress Reports also help to keep stakeholders informed of progress and needs for additional support. By sharing this information, it can build support and help cultivate champions for the effort within the organization.

HOW: Refer to Chapter 3 in **Boomer Volunteer Engagement** for instructions on how to complete a Progress Report. Following the Work Session, members of the Task Force should work together to complete this form and submit it to the co-facilitators prior to the next Work Session. This can also be shared with organizational leaders (the executive, the Board, or others who are tracking progress on this initiative and providing support).

PROGRESS REPORT

Vision: _____

Element	Description	Indicators and Tools	Progress, Challenges, and Needs
Resources			
Action			
Yield			
Initial Impact			
Sustained Outcome			

Co-Facilitator Work Session Report

WHAT: This is an assessment tool for the co-facilitators to use following each Task Force Work Session to reflect on their facilitation and to track their own progress as facilitators.

WHY: Taking time to reflect on these questions following each Work Session will ensure that the co-facilitators stay in tune with each other, identify successful facilitation tactics, and strategize ways to improve where needed. This process can also help to keep stakeholders informed of progress and needs for additional support. By sharing this information, it can build support and help cultivate champions for the effort within the organization.

HOW: Following the Work Session, the two co-facilitators should sit down to complete this form jointly and discuss the answers openly and honestly. This can also be shared with organizational leaders (the executive, the Board, or others who are tracking progress on this initiative and providing support).

Co-Facilitator Work Session Report

Use this form to record the results of your meetings with the Task Force.

Co-facilitators _____

Organization _____

Meeting Date _____ Time _____

Attended by _____

Did we complete the agenda? (If no, what sections were not covered and why?) _____
_____

_____

What issues or questions were raised? _____
_____

_____

What were the successes of this meeting? _____
_____

_____

What were the challenges? _____
_____

_____

What are our next steps? _____
_____

_____

How can we work together to keep the endeavor moving forward? Do we need any additional support? If so, what is our plan to request that support?
_____

_____

_____

_____

MODULE 6

Task Force Work Session 4

Launching the Pilot and Tracking Progress

KEY OUTCOMES

As a result of this Work Session, participants will:

1. Benchmark progress with the co-facilitators.

2. Share challenges and receive feedback and coaching on how to address their challenges.

Related Material in *Boomer Volunteer Engagement*:

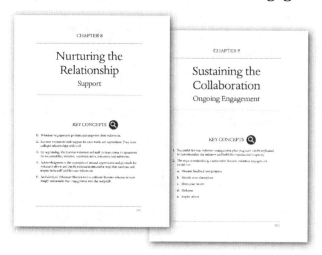

[THE FRAMEWORK]

The Work Plan is in place, volunteers have been cultivated, and the pilot has been launched. Now it is time to truly support the team. One of the most important elements to providing meaningful support is to measure progress. Performance measurement is important to quantify impacts and outcomes – to tell the story of what the program accomplishes. Performance measurement is also key to identifying how to best support the volunteers and staff who are implementing the process.

Performance measurement, also known as "outcomes-based assessment," is the system of ongoing monitoring and reporting of program accomplishments, particularly progress toward pre-established goals. Together, the Work Plan and the Progress Reports are your performance measurement tools. As noted earlier, the Progress Report is a way for the Task Force to systematically track accomplishments and avoid being surprised by progress or problems. The Progress Report is the mechanism to ensure that the Task Force is communicating with the volunteers and staff who are implementing the Work Plan. Communicating about both the progress and the problems will empower the Task Force to intervene early when needed to provide resources, solutions, and other support to address problems and keep the initiative moving forward.

⚙️ TOOLS

- Agenda for Task Force Work Session 4
- Task Force Progress Report
- Co-Facilitator Work Session Report

✓ MAKING IT HAPPEN

- Hold the fourth Task Force Work Session, focusing on the pilot launch and have the Task Force track progress of the project in comparison to the Work Plan.
- At the conclusion of the Work Session, both the Task Force and the co-facilitators should track their progress using the appropriate tracking tools and identify action steps to address any emerging problems:
  – **Task Force Progress Report**
  – **Co-Facilitator Work Session Report**

Agenda for Work Session 4
Launching the Pilot and Tracking Progress

WHAT: This is an agenda for the fourth Work Session of the Task Force. Work Session 4 should be scheduled for 1.5 to 2 hours.

WHY: The purpose of this meeting is to benchmark progress, identify any obstacles needing to be addressed, and establish a plan of action to address them.

HOW: Use this agenda to plan and guide the Task Force Work Session.

Launching the Pilot and Tracking Progress

Participants
Co-facilitators
Task Force Members

Meeting Length
1.5 to 2 hours

Prep Work
One week prior to this meeting, the Task Force members should submit an updated **Progress Report** to the Co-Facilitators to report their progress, challenges, and adjustments to the plan.

🏵 DISCUSSION GUIDE

I. Checking on Progress

- Are we on track with our Work Plan? Why, why not?
- At this point, the organization should have cultivated, interviewed, and selected volunteers for the new positions and should have begun implementing the Work Plan. If we have not reached this point, what challenges are we encountering? What would help address those challenges and move the project forward? How can the co-facilitators help? How can organizational leaders help? For example, perhaps the new volunteer position has been posted on several volunteer matching sites and Task Force members have made requests to potential volunteers, but the postings and meetings have not attracted interested volunteers. How can the position description be reevaluated and revised? Does it have the right title? Is the position actually do-able? How can the position description be revised to be more appealing and still meet our goals?
- Does the Work Plan need to be revised to reflect a new timeline?
- In which aspects of the project are we finding success? Why?

- Which aspects of the project are we finding challenging? Why? How will we address these challenges?

II. Reflecting on the Shift towards Volunteer Engagement

- How has your role as staff or volunteers changed through this process thus far?

III. Next Steps

Remind the Task Force of the time and location of the next meeting and ask them to do the following in preparation for that meeting:
- Update the Progress Report

Task Force Progress Report

WHAT: This is a tracking tool for the Task Force members to use following each Task Force Work Session to reflect on their progress in implementing their Work Plan.

WHY: Benchmarking progress is important to ensure continued forward movement as well as to identify roadblocks and strategize effective ways to move beyond them. Progress Reports prevent unexpected surprises from derailing the entire initiative by alerting team members early on and enabling them to be nimble and flexible in finding ways to achieve the intended results. They help inform the co-facilitators of emerging issues so the Work Sessions can be tailored to address them. Progress Reports also help to keep stakeholders informed of progress and needs for additional support. By sharing this information, it can build support and help cultivate champions for the effort within the organization.

HOW: Refer to Chapter 3 in *Boomer Volunteer Engagement* for instructions on how to complete a Progress Report. Following the Work Session, members of the Task Force should work together to complete this form and submit it to the co-facilitators prior to the next Work Session. This can also be shared with organizational leaders (the executive, the Board, or others who are tracking progress on this initiative and providing support).

PROGRESS REPORT

Vision: _____

Element	Description	Indicators and Tools	Progress, Challenges, and Needs
Resources			
Action			
Yield			
Initial Impact			
Sustained Outcome			

Co-Facilitator Work Session Report

WHAT: This is an assessment tool for the co-facilitators to use following each Task Force Work Session to reflect on their facilitation and to track their own progress as facilitators.

WHY: Taking time to reflect on these questions following each Work Session will ensure that the co-facilitators stay in tune with each other, identify successful facilitation tactics, and strategize ways to improve where needed. This process can also help to keep stakeholders informed of progress and needs for additional support. By sharing this information, it can build support and help cultivate champions for the effort within the organization.

HOW: Following the Work Session, the two co-facilitators should sit down to complete this form jointly and discuss the answers openly and honestly. This can also be shared with organizational leaders (the executive, the Board, or others who are tracking progress on this initiative and providing support).

Co-Facilitator Work Session Report

Use this form to record the results of your meetings with the Task Force.

Co-Facilitators _____

Organization _____

Meeting Date _____ Time _____

Attended by _____

Did we complete the agenda? (If no, what sections were not covered and why?) _____

_____

_____

What issues or questions were raised? _____

_____

_____

What were the successes of this meeting? _____

_____

_____

What were the challenges? _____

_____

_____

What are our next steps? _____

_____

_____

How can we work together to keep the endeavor moving forward? Do we need any additional support? If so, what is our plan to request that support?

_____

_____

_____

_____

NOTES & IDEAS

Task Force Work Session 5

Tracking Progress and Preparing to Wrap-Up

KEY OUTCOMES

As a result of this Work Session, participants will:

1. Benchmark progress with the co-facilitators.

2. Share challenges and receive feedback and coaching on how to address these challenges.

3. Prepare to wrap up the program and integrate these techniques into long-term practices and identify key stakeholders who would have valuable input in the evaluation process.

Related Material in *Boomer Volunteer Engagement*:

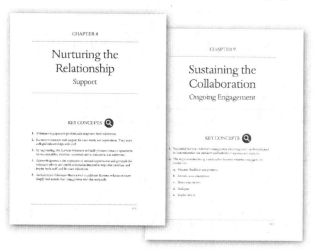

[THE FRAMEWORK]

As the project is implemented, the Task Force continues to focus on monitoring progress. As mentioned in Module 6, performance measurement is a system of regularly measuring project accomplishments with an eye to ensuring that the actual outcomes match the intended goals. In other words, are you achieving what you set out to achieve? Whether the answer is "yes" or "no," the process is an important learning opportunity.

When the project is on track, the Task Force should reflect on what circumstances were in place to leverage the project for success. How has each person contributed to the successes thus far? What actions or communications have helped others be receptive and supportive of this project? What strategies have been implemented to clear the way for this new initiative to keep moving forward? And, most importantly, how has the Task Force's planning helped to lay out an effective plan of action?

Of course, at this point in the process, performance measurement may reveal that the project is not on track. This, too, is an important learning opportunity. The Task Force's role is to identify where the project has veered off course and make needed corrections. What are the problems or delays? Does the pilot need some re-engineering to produce the intended impacts and outcomes? What tactics could help get the project back on course? What communications will help? Are additional resources needed?

7

When challenges arise, it is important to brainstorm solutions while the work is still ongoing, rather than waiting until the project is complete. Making mid-course corrections is how an organization learns to be nimble, to take risks, and to reinforce the spirit of innovation.

Identifying all of these issues through systematic performance measurement will be very useful when the Task Force evaluates the project overall (Module 8). When the team seeks to identify which program elements should be replicated in order to make wider organizational change, these Progress Reports will provide valuable information about what has worked well, where challenges have arisen, and which tactics were effective in addressing those challenges.

✿✿ TOOLS

- Agenda for Task Force Work Session 5
- Assessment of Organizational Volunteer Engagement
- Task Force Progress Report
- Co-Facilitator Work Session Report

✓ MAKING IT HAPPEN

- Hold the fifth Task Force Work Session, focusing on pilot implementation and tracking its progress against the Work Plan.
- Set the stage for the Task Force to begin reflecting on the success and challenges in this pilot in order to do a systematic evaluation at the final Work Session.
- At the conclusion of the Work Session, both the Task Force and the co-facilitators should track their progress using the appropriate tracking tools:
  - **Task Force Progress Report**
  - **Co-Facilitator Work Session Report**

Agenda for Work Session 5
Tracking Progress and Preparing to Wrap-Up

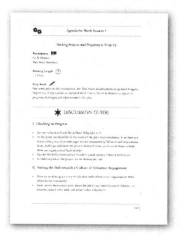

WHAT: This is an agenda for the fifth Work Session of the Task Force. Work Session 5 should be scheduled to last at least 1.5 hours.

WHY: The purpose of this meeting is to benchmark progress and identify any obstacles needing to be addressed.

HOW: Use this agenda to plan and guide the Task Force Work Session.

Tracking Progress and Preparing to Wrap-Up

Participants

Co-facilitators

Task Force Members

Meeting Length

1.5 hours

Prep Work 🖊

One week prior to this consultation, the Task Force should submit an updated Progress Report and, if appropriate, an updated Work Plan to the co-facilitators to report its progress, challenges, and adjustments to the plan.

✸ DISCUSSION GUIDE

I. Checking on Progress

- Are we on track with our Work Plan? Why, why not?
- At this point, we should be in the midst of the pilot implementation. If we have not reached this point, what challenges are we encountering? What would help address those challenges and move the project forward? How can the co-facilitators help? How can organizational leaders help?
- Has the Work Plan been revised to reflect a new timeline? Does it need to be?
- In which aspects of the project are we finding success?

II. Fueling the Shift towards a Culture of Volunteer Engagement

- How are we sharing the story of this pilot with others in our organization? With others in our community?
- How can we share information about the pilot's successes thus far to inform constituents, inspire other staff, and attract other volunteers?

- How has our role as staff or volunteers changed through this process thus far? Are we sharing some of this learning with others? How?

III. Preparing for Evaluation

What other key stakeholders should be invited to participate in the sixth Work Session, which will focus on evaluating the pilot? Consider Board members, representatives from partner organizations, and others who could provide evaluative feedback or have ideas for the next volunteer engagement initiatives.

IV. Next Steps

Remind the Task Force of the time and location of the next meeting and ask them to do the following in preparation for that meeting:

- Update the Progress Report.
- Complete the **Assessment of Organizational Volunteer Engagement** once again. This is a document they will have completed prior to starting this program and, by filling it out again, they will be able to track the areas of change and impact on their volunteer engagement practices.
- Review the list of other key stakeholders and invite them to participate in the sixth Work Session.

Assessment of Organizational Volunteer Engagement

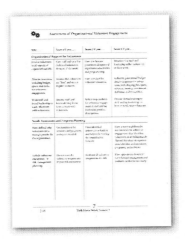

WHAT: This assessment was originally completed by Task Force members prior to the first Task Force Work Session. The Task Force is asked to complete it again now that the pilot project has been launched.

WHY: When the Task Force first completed this Assessment roughly five months ago, the results provided a snapshot of the organization's volunteer engagement practices and pointed to areas of strength and opportunity. Since then, the Task Force has launched a pilot project and begun building momentum towards a culture of volunteer engagement. By completing this Assessment again, the Task Force will be able to track areas of change in the organization's volunteer engagement practices.

HOW: Prior to the last Task Force work session, have all the Task Force members complete this Assessment and bring their results to the Work Session for discussion. Be sure to bring the original Assessment results to the meeting as well.

YOU . . .	Score 1 if you . . .	Score 2 if you . . .	Score 3 if you . . .
Organizational Support for Volunteers			
Involve volunteers in all aspects of organizational life.	Have staff and/or a few dedicated volunteers do most of the work.	Have a volunteer presence in all aspects of organizational activities and programming.	Mandate that staff and leadership utilize volunteers in their work.
Allocate resources, including budget, space, and tools, for volunteer engagement.	Assume that volunteers are "free" and do not require resources.	Have a budget for volunteer resources.	Reflect in your annual budget detailed expenses for volunteers, including supplies, space, software, training, recruitment, staff time, and recognition.
Train staff and board leadership to work effectively with volunteers.	Assume staff and key leadership know how to work with volunteers.	Reflect responsibility for volunteer engagement in staff and lay leadership position descriptions.	Provide formal training to staff and lay leadership on how to work with volunteers.
Needs Assessment and Program Planning			
Have defined why volunteers are a strategic priority for the organization.	Use volunteers for activities and programs as they are needed.	Have identified volunteers as leaders and helpers in moving the organization forward.	Have a written philosophy statement about volunteer engagement that identifies volunteers as an indispensable channel for ideas on organizational direction and operations, programs, and activities.
Include volunteer engagement in risk management planning.	Do not consider volunteer assignments in your risk assessment.	Evaluate all volunteer assignments for risk.	Have appropriate insurance for volunteer engagement and evaluate/update as necessary.

YOU . . .	Score 1 if you . . .	Score 2 if you . . .	Score 3 if you . . .
Effective Recruitment and Cultivation			
Have written position descriptions for all volunteer assignments.	Verbally explain to volunteers what they are going to do.	Have a position description for each volunteer assignment.	Conduct an annual (at minimum) review and update of all position descriptions.
Have a process for volunteer cultivation.	Do recruitment exclusively through announcements in the newsletter, website postings, etc.	Figure out who knows prospective volunteers and have them do the recruiting.	Have a written strategic recruitment plan for all volunteer assignments and needs.
Maintain current and accurate records on volunteers.	Do not track volunteer involvement.	Have a record of all volunteers and what they do for the organization.	Integrate volunteer records with membership and donor information.
Interviewing and Placement			
Design volunteer assignments for a wide range of skills, ages, and interests.	Rely on a specific group of volunteers (e.g., stay-at-home mothers, retired, etc.) to get the work done.	Include all age groups and demographics among your volunteers.	Design assignments specifically to reflect a wide range of skills and interests and not limit work to clerical and administrative positions.
Screen and place volunteers in assignments that are right for them and the organization.	Let anyone volunteer for anything.	Match volunteers to the assignment that aligns with their interests.	Recruit volunteers based on their preferences, the skills they willingly share, and the relevant qualifications for the job.
Orientation and Planning			
Have written policies and procedures for volunteer engagement.	Assume that volunteers know what is acceptable for them to do.	Have some policies that relate to volunteer involvement.	Have detailed written policies and procedures and orient all volunteers to these guidelines.

YOU . . .	Score 1 if you . . .	Score 2 if you . . .	Score 3 if you . . .
Supervision and Support			
Hold volunteers accountable for what they do.	Cannot fire a volunteer.	Clarify for volunteers the limits and boundaries of their assignments.	Have staff and leadership follow up with volunteers to make sure they accomplish what they set out to do, releasing them as needed.
Actively solicit volunteer input in decisions that affect them.	Have volunteers do whatever they are assigned.	Encourage current volunteers to give feedback.	Have a system in place for collecting and reflecting on volunteer feedback on decisions that affect them.
Strategies for Sustainability (Retention)			
Have volunteer assignments that are meaningful and that impact the ability of the organization to achieve its mission.	Design volunteer assignments around having people do the work of the staff and/ or board of directors.	Design volunteer assignments to have an impact on the mission of the organization.	Reflect a diversity of work in volunteer assignments, from direct service to program delivery, and incorporate high-level assignments, such as the provision of professional services.
Ensure that staff and leadership recognize volunteers informally and formally.	Host an annual recognition event for volunteers.	Give frequent recognition to volunteers from the board, staff, and other volunteer leaders.	Acknowledge the successes of volunteer endeavors in personalized ways through sharing celebratory information in collateral materials (e.g., the website, newsletters, announcements, emails, and written materials), through letters, and through customized networking opportunities with organizational leaders and others.

To score your answers, see page 85.

Task Force Progress Report

WHAT: This is a tracking tool for the Task Force members to use following each Task Force Work Session to reflect on their progress in implementing their Work Plan.

WHY: Benchmarking progress is important to ensure continued forward movement as well as to identify roadblocks and strategize effective ways to move beyond them. Progress Reports prevent unexpected surprises from derailing the entire initiative by alerting team members early on and enabling them to be nimble and flexible in finding ways to achieve the intended results. They help inform the co-facilitators of emerging issues so the Work Sessions can be tailored to address them. Progress Reports also help to keep stakeholders informed of progress and needs for additional support. By sharing this information, it can build support and help cultivate champions for the effort within the organization.

HOW: Refer to Chapter 3 in *Boomer Volunteer Engagement* for instructions on how to complete a Progress Report. Following the Work Session, members of the Task Force should work together to complete this form and submit it to the co-facilitators prior to the next Work Session. This can also be shared with organizational leaders (the executive, the Board, or others who are tracking progress on this initiative and providing support).

PROGRESS REPORT

Vision: _____

Element	Description	Indicators and Tools	Progress, Challenges, and Needs
Resources			
Action			
Yield			
Initial Impact			
Sustained Outcome			

Co-Facilitator Work Session Report

WHAT: This is an assessment tool for the co-facilitators to use following each Task Force Work Session to reflect on their facilitation and to track their own progress as facilitators.

WHY: Taking time to reflect on these questions following each Work Session will ensure that the co-facilitators stay in tune with each other, identify successful facilitation tactics, and strategize ways to improve where needed. This process can also help to keep stakeholders informed of progress and needs for additional support. By sharing this information, it can build support and help cultivate champions for the effort within the organization.

HOW: Following the Work Session, the two co-facilitators should sit down to complete this form jointly and discuss the answers openly and honestly. This can also be shared with organizational leaders (the executive, the Board, or others who are tracking progress on this initiative and providing support).

Co-Facilitator Work Session Report

Use this form to record the results of your meetings with the Task Force.

Co-Facilitators _____

Organization _____

Meeting Date _____ Time _____

Attended by _____

Did we complete the agenda? (If no, what sections were not covered and why?) _____

_____

_____

What issues or questions were raised? _____

_____

_____

What were the successes of this meeting? _____

_____

_____

What were the challenges? _____

_____

_____

What are our next steps? _____

_____

_____

How can we work together to keep the endeavor moving forward? Do we need any additional support? If so, what is our plan to request that support?

_____

_____

_____

_____

NOTES & IDEAS

Task Force Work Session 6
Documenting the Program and Sustaining the Culture

KEY OUTCOMES

As a result of this Work Session, participants will:

1. Explicitly identify the impacts of this project and document the challenges and accomplishments.

2. Through documentation of project impacts, create institutional knowledge that will drive efficiency and position future initiatives for success.

3. Develop strategies to sustain high-impact volunteer engagement with the organization.

4. Understand the Task Force's next steps as they wrap up their involvement with the project.

[THE FRAMEWORK]

The pilot process enables an organization to experiment with innovation and build momentum toward larger cultural change. Innovation is also a process that continues beyond the initial experiment and includes taking the time to review the initial project, assess its success and shortcomings, adjust the project in response to the assessment, and make an informed plan about how (or if) to continue the endeavor.

Sustaining innovation means taking the time to:

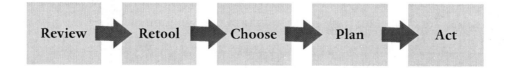

Review → Retool → Choose → Plan → Act

Only after completing these steps are you, as an organization, able to grow by leveraging this momentum to replicate successful pilots, initiate new pilots, access newly acquired skills and competencies, and more. In other words, it is a continuous cycle:

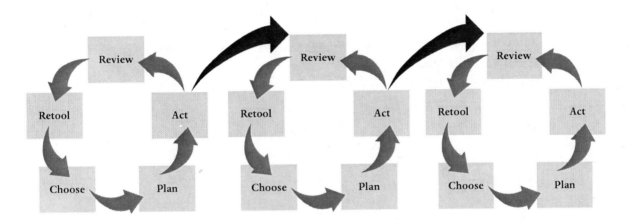

Use the **Next Steps of Innovation** tool as the Task Force reviews, retools, chooses, and plans for your next act.

⚙⚙ TOOLS

- Agenda for Work Session 6
- Pilot Evaluation
- Needs Assessment, including the results from the Needs Assessment originally completed in Work Session 1
- Pilot Project Selection Questions
- Work Plan
- Task Force Progress Report
- Co-Facilitator Work Session Report

- Hold the sixth Task Force Work Session, focusing on evaluating the pilot success and on using that information to begin developing strategies to plan for future innovations.
- Utilize the **Pilot Evaluation** to guide the discussion, inform decisions about future actions, and fuel the momentum towards a culture of volunteer engagement.
- At the conclusion of the Work Session, both the Task Force and the co-facilitators should track their progress using the appropriate tracking tools:
  - **Task Force Progress Report**
  - **Co-Facilitator Work Session Report**

Agenda for Work Session 6:
Documenting the Program and Sustaining the Culture

WHAT: This is an agenda for the sixth Work Session of the Task Force. Because this session focuses on evaluating months of work as well as planning for future volunteer engagement initiatives, Work Session 6 should be scheduled to last at least 2 hours.

WHY: By systematically evaluating the impacts of the pilot project, the Task Force will be better able to develop strategies to sustain high-impact volunteer engagement with the organization.

HOW: Use this agenda to plan and guide the Task Force Work Session.

Documenting the Program and Sustaining the Culture

Participants
Co-facilitators
Task Force Members
Key stakeholders, including Board members, representatives from partner organizations, and others who can provide evaluative feedback or have ideas for the next volunteer engagement initiatives

Meeting Length
2 hours

Prep Work
Each member of the Task Force should have completed the Assessment of Organizational Volunteer Engagement and bring those results to the Work Session.

Additionally, the Task Force should make sure that the pilot Work Plan and all Progress Reports are accurate and up to date. Co-facilitators should provide copies of these documents as well as copies of the original **Needs Assessment** results to all Task Force members so they can review these materials prior to this Work Session.

DISCUSSION GUIDE

The cycle of innovation involves five key steps. In order to create sustainable change, the organization should:

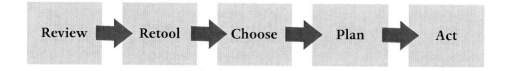

At this Work Session, we will begin to address all of these important steps.

I. Review

Exercise: Pilot Evaluation ⚙⚙

- In a group, complete **Step 1** of the **Pilot Evaluation**. If a large group, break into smaller groups for this exercise, then reconvene and compare answers.
- Complete **Step 2: Next Steps** as a group.

Additional Questions for Discussion

- What were the measurable successes from this program?
- After reviewing the recently completed **Assessment of Organizational Volunteer Engagement** and comparing it to the original one (completed at the beginning of the program), how have our volunteer engagement practices changed? In what area(s) did we make the greatest shift? What were the results of that shift?
- How have others in our organization reacted to this project?
- How have we documented the successes and challenges? Have we shared this project with the other staff? With the Board? With other volunteers? With our organizational constituents? With our funders?

II. Retool

Looking at the "Adjustments" column of the **Pilot Evaluation** in particular, what changes ought to be implemented? (Possibilities include updating position descriptions, revising the timeline, cultivating new team members, and more.)

Additional Questions for Discussion

- How can we continue to engage new volunteers with our organization? How can we use these volunteers (and others) to cultivate additional skilled volunteers to meet emerging needs?

III. Choose

- We now have the information we need to determine the future of the pilot. Remember, our options include not only continuation or replication, but also suspending the program, continuing only a portion of it, turning it over to a self-directed team, and many other possibilities.

- In order to determine our next steps, we should start by reviewing our organizational needs.

Exercise: Needs Assessment Update ✿✿

Review the Needs Assessment that the Task Force completed at the first Work Session and update the answers, considering what has changed in the organization and in the world since they first completed it.

Exercise: Pilot Project Selection Questions ✿✿

With the updated Needs Assessment and the list of recommended changes to the pilot project in mind, brainstorm a list of options for another pilot initiative to harness the momentum created by the first pilot project. Using the **Pilot Project Selection Questions** as a filter once again, which options will be the best investment of our time and resources?

Additional Questions to Consider

- Who else in the organization can use a skilled, high-impact volunteer?
- Is there another emerging need that could be addressed through Boomer Volunteer Engagement?
- What steps do we need to take to make that happen?

IV. Plan

Exercise: Work Plan ✿✿

Once the next pilot project is selected, a new **Work Plan** should be developed. It is important that we plan our next endeavor as carefully and intentionally as we did the first pilot. What have we learned from the initial pilot project that should be incorporated into this endeavor? Which new skills and competencies? What new resources? Who should be involved now? How does this impact Task Force composition?

V. Act

Make a plan to launch the initiative. With this plan, the cycle continues and the organization is ever closer to becoming a nimble, responsive organization harnessing the abundance of its volunteer resource.

Pilot Evaluation

WHAT: This tool is designed to help all stakeholders evaluate the success of the pilot project and its implications for future volunteer engagement innovations.

WHY: The results of this evaluation discussion will inform the organization's decisions about what actions to take and which strategies to employ to build a culture of volunteer engagement.

HOW: Break the Work Session participants up into small groups and have each complete this exercise. Reconvene the groups and share results. After comparing answers to the chart, address the final questions as a group.

Pilot _____ Date _____

Preparation: Prior to completing this exercise, the pilot Work Plan and all Progress Reports should be accurate and up to date. All meeting participants should have reviewed these materials before this discussion.

Step 2: Identifying Next Steps
In small groups, complete the chart below.

Area for Review	Evaluation How did it go?	Adjustments What changes are needed to make this sustainable and successful in the future?
Planning and Timing Were the resources listed on the Work Plan correct and complete?		
Were the position descriptions on target?		
Did we have all the necessary competencies on our team?		
How accurate was the timeline?		
If there were delays, what caused them?		
If we had more time or less time, would we have had different results?		

Area for Review	Evaluation How did it go?	Adjustments What changes are needed to make this sustainable and successful in the future?
Human Capital Did our team/organization have the skills needed to successfully complete the pilot?		
What new skills were gained by those who participated in the pilot?		
Who emerged through this process as new leaders? As potential leaders for future initiatives? As champions for volunteer engagement?		
How could the project have benefitted from additional human resources?		

Area for Review	Evaluation How did it go?	Adjustments What changes are needed to make this sustainable and successful in the future?
Results Did our actions directly advance our goals?		
What unintended results occurred? (Think in terms of beneficiaries, the organization's reputation, financial resources, partnerships, etc.)		
Are we closer to effecting our original vision for innovation? In what ways, or why not? What new story was told by this pilot?		
Who has heard the story of this pilot so far?		
Who still needs to hear this story?		

Step 2: Identifying Next Steps

We now have the information we need to decide how to move forward. Do we continue this pilot with some adjustments, perhaps expanding or replicating it? Do we continue all or pieces of it in a different form? Do we complete it and apply the lessons learned and new resources toward our next innovation? Do we have other options?

Needs Assessment

WHAT: This is an assessment tool to help Task Force members reflect on what could be done at the organization if there were more resources available.

WHY: Task Force members completed this assessment during Work Session 1. Repeating the process at this point enables the team to use emerging needs and current trends to help select the next project.

HOW: Have individuals complete this assessment individually, then discuss as a group.

1. What are the dreams for our organization that require more people, expertise, money, or tools to accomplish?

2. What are the problems and challenges that our organization is currently experiencing?

3. What is our organization currently doing that we would like to increase, replicate, or expand?

4. What is an area of your division/ department that is always underutilized or understaffed, or seems constantly overloaded?

5. What specific skills and resources would our organization's personnel need to fulfill your dreams? To meet its challenges?

6. Who in our circles of influence embraces volunteers and would be open to building the organization's capacity to address these dreams and challenges?

7. Who are our Mavens? Who are the
   experts on volunteering? Who are the
   experts on projects your organization
   wants to begin or complete?

8. Who are our Connectors? Who seems
   connected to everyone in particular
   communities you want to tap? (Which
   communities?)

9. Who are our Salespeople? Who can sell
   someone the shirt off her back and
   make her glad to buy it?

10. Are you an answer to any of the previous three questions? (Which ones? Why?)

_____

_____

_____

_____

_____

_____

_____

11. With what could our organization utilize a consultant or specialist to help us—now and in the future—work toward vision and mission fulfillment?

_____

_____

_____

_____

_____

_____

_____

12. What areas of our organization would benefit from program outcome evaluation?

_____

_____

_____

_____

_____

_____

_____

Based on these Needs Assessment data, what are three entrepreneurial volunteer assignments or volunteer leadership positions that would be an asset to our organization?

1. _____

2. _____

3. _____

Pilot Project Selection Questions

WHAT: This is a discussion tool to use to help select the focus of the next pilot program.

WHY: As with the first pilot, ensuring that your next project is leveraged for success is important to creating a sustainable culture of volunteer engagement.

HOW: Review the list of possible projects and use the Pilot Project Selection Questions to discuss which project will be selected for implementation.

For each possible pilot project, consider these questions and use the answers to determine whether this is the best way to intervene with strategic volunteer engagement.

Potential Pilot Project _____

Does it play to strength? _____

Will it come as a surprise to any key stakeholders? _____

What changes to current practice are needed? _____

_____

_____

_____

Do existing volunteers and staff have the expertise and time to carry this out – or need to be trained?

_____

Are more or different people needed? _____

Are new position descriptions needed? _____

What are the biggest anticipated challenges? _____

_____

_____

_____

What are you willing to invest? _____

_____

_____

_____

What aren't you willing to invest? _____

_____

_____

_____

Is it sustainable? _____

Work Plan

WHAT: This is a template for the Work Plan that will outline the scope of the project.

WHY: A Work Plan establishes the vision and impact of the project, outlines key action steps, and provides indicators against which leaders can measure progress.

HOW: Refer to Chapter 3 in **Boomer Volunteer Engagement** for detailed instructions on how to complete a Work Plan and to see sample Work Plans.

⚙⚙ Work Plan

Vision Statement	Resources	Action	Yield	Initial Impact	Sustained Outcome

Task Force Progress Report

WHAT: This is a tracking tool for the Task Force members to use following each Task Force Work Session to reflect on their progress in implementing their Work Plan.

WHY: Benchmarking progress is important to ensure continued forward movement as well as to identify roadblocks and strategize effective ways to move beyond them. Progress Reports prevent unexpected surprises from derailing the entire initiative by alerting team members early on and enabling them to be nimble and flexible in finding ways to achieve the intended results. They help inform the co-facilitators of emerging issues so the Work Sessions can be tailored to address them. Progress Reports also help to keep stakeholders informed of progress and needs for additional support. By sharing this information, it can build support and help cultivate champions for the effort within the organization.

HOW: Refer to Chapter 3 in *Boomer Volunteer Engagement* for instructions on how to complete a Progress Report. Following the Work Session, members of the Task Force should work together to complete this form and submit it to the co-facilitators prior to the next Work Session. This can also be shared with organizational leaders (the executive, the Board, or others who are tracking progress on this initiative and providing support).

PROGRESS REPORT

Vision: _____

Element	Description	Indicators and Tools	Progress, Challenges, and Needs
Resources			
Action			
Yield			
Initial Impact			
Sustained Outcome			

Co-Facilitator Work Session Report

WHAT: This is an assessment tool for the co-facilitators to use following each Task Force Work Session to reflect on their facilitation and to track their own progress as facilitators.

WHY: Taking time to reflect on these questions following each Work Session will ensure that the co-facilitators stay in tune with each other, identify successful facilitation tactics, and strategize ways to improve where needed. This process can also help to keep stakeholders informed of progress and needs for additional support. By sharing this information, it can build support and help cultivate champions for the effort within the organization.

HOW: Following the Work Session, the two co-facilitators should sit down to complete this form jointly and discuss the answers openly and honestly. This can also be shared with organizational leaders (the executive, the Board, or others who are tracking progress on this initiative and providing support).

Co-Facilitator Work Session Report

Use this form to record the results of your meetings with the Task Force.

Co-Facilitators _____

Organization _____

Meeting Date _____ Time _____

Attended by _____

Did we complete the agenda? (If no, what sections were not covered and why?) _____

_____

_____

What issues or questions were raised? _____

_____

_____

What were the successes of this meeting? _____

_____

_____

What were the challenges? _____

_____

_____

What are our next steps? _____

_____

_____

How can we work together to keep the endeavor moving forward? Do we need any additional
support? If so, what is our plan to request that support?

_____

_____

_____

_____

8

NOTES & IDEAS

Epilogue

March 2010

Much has changed in the volunteer landscape since we completed *Boomer Volunteer Engagement: Collaborate Today, Thrive Tomorrow* in March of 2008 – and most of the changes have only underscored the importance of re-engineering the way we engage volunteers for greater strategic impact. When we began writing that book in 2007, the dialogue in the volunteer world was about Baby Boomers advancing to retirement and what nonprofits would need to do differently to engage them. We found that discussion compelling enough to write the book on the wave of enthusiasm and interest in engaging the skills, talents, and circles of influence of the Baby Boomer generation.

Just two years later, the conversation in the volunteer world has changed dramatically. The economic downturn starting in August 2008 and continuing into 2010 has profoundly impacted the national conversation about volunteerism. Several national studies report increases in volunteerism. Most notably, the Corporation for National & Community Service study, *Volunteering in America 2009*, and the Bureau of Labor Statistics report, *Volunteering in the United States 2009*, both document steady increases in volunteering, especially by women volunteers and individuals aged 35 to 54. Most notably, volunteerism has become "cool," as described in *The Chronicle of Philanthropy* article, "10 Emerging Forces in 2010"[2]. And, people view volunteerism as a real solution that can make a difference in their communities and in the world. According to a *Parade Magazine* poll,

---

2 Chronicle of Philanthropy, "10 Emerging Forces in 2010," December 10, 2009, http://philanthropy.com/article/10-Emerging-Forces-in-2010/57633/. (accessed March 16, 2010).

people believe volunteerism is important, that the actions of one person can improve the world, and that they are more involved than their parents were in making a difference.[3] In this report, public service is described as a "way of life for Americans of all ages." Patrick Corvington, CEO of the Corporation for National & Community Service, states:

> *I think that part of what is driving the overall increase is the*
> *growing understanding that service is an essential tool to achieve*
> *community and national goals.*

Many factors have contributed to this new laser-like focus on volunteerism and service. The 2008 Presidential campaign engaged millions of Americans as activists through the internet and social networking. The passage of the Edward M. Kennedy Serve America Act in March 2009 and the expansion of AmeriCorps have created greater interest in national service. With the rise in unemployment, large numbers of unemployed and underemployed Americans have chosen to volunteer while they are seeking work, finding volunteering a way to stay connected, keep up existing skills, and learn new ones. Corporations have jumped on the bandwagon with unprecedented focus through such campaigns as iParticipate, Disney's "Give a Day, Get a Disney Day," and the American Express Members Project, which have brought legions of Americans to service.

The economic downturn has been hard on nonprofit organizations. Layoffs, furloughs, and hiring freezes are commonplace. Prior to August of 2008, when nonprofits wanted to grow capacity, they hired more staff; when they wanted to create new programs, they hired even more staff. Those days are gone, at least for the foreseeable future. It is in this dramatic economic environment that volunteerism is flourishing. In this new atmosphere of increased focus on volunteer engagement and a strong ethic of volunteerism, many organizations have chosen to rethink their volunteer strategies. Their courage, tenacity, and willingness to embrace change have been profoundly inspirational to us. They are actively seizing the moment and capitalizing on the volunteerism trend to build their organizational capacity. These organizational leaders know that the role of change agent in bureaucratic organizations is challenging, yet they describe the rewards as being incalculable.

---

3 Berland, Michael. "Compassion Counts More Than Ever." *Parade Magazine*, March 7, 2010. http://www.parade.com/news/what-america-cares-about/featured/100307-compassion-counts-more-than-ever.html (accessed March 22, 2010).

We have seen our clients accomplish a great deal, often in less than six months. Here are a few of the outcomes they have achieved:

- Increased ability to be nimble and flexible to meet the demands of new economic realities.
- Improved aptitude to cultivate new enthusiastic advocates for their organizations.
- Increased employee satisfaction as they are now focusing on the work that is best suited to them.
- Understanding volunteerism as a core business strategy to survive and thrive no matter the external environment.
- Enhanced status and importance of volunteerism within their organizations and expanded circles of influence outside their organizations.
- New programs and services that would not be possible without volunteers and volunteer leaders.
- Ability to be more responsive to stakeholder and community needs because they have the organizational capacity to make this possible.

We have learned much over the last two years about the value of innovation, change, and engagement. Here are a few things we found most valuable:

- Moving volunteers from a peripheral program to an organization-wide strategy benefits stakeholders and the communities served.
- Learning new strategies for change impacts all of the organization, not just volunteers. It helps the organization to be nimble and flexible to address all challenges it encounters.
- Honoring traditional and current volunteers helps to avoid dissonance in the change process. Inviting them to participate in change and organizational development means volunteers can opt in or opt out. When change is piloted in small, manageable increments, most accept it as an experiment, and, ultimately, when it is successful, more people will opt in.
- Changing the culture of volunteer engagement works well in both small and large organizations. Small organizations often move faster at the start when implementing change. Nevertheless, all of the large organizations with whom we have worked catch up to the pace of change within 12 to 18 months. While it takes longer to turn a larger ship, the results are just as dramatic.

- Support from the top executives and the Board of Directors is critical to success. When organizational leaders model the change they want to see, change happens. Without them, change becomes ephemeral, just the flavor of the day and other emerging organizational priorities will win out.
- Starting small to transform the culture of volunteer engagement is very important. Thinking too big does not result in bigger results. In fact, it often results in frustration and the need to revise Work Plans and strategies.
- Volunteer initiatives can, and often do, lead the way for change in other parts of the organization. As momentum builds, the organization is better able to embrace change on many levels.
- The pilot approach works. It allows for greater risk tolerance and the ability to experiment without threatening the way of life of an organization.
- Embracing change and recognizing the abundant resources already within an organization's reach are very powerful decisions. Once you decide to encourage change and acknowledge the abundance, you have the courage and confidence to try new solutions and employ alternatives practices.

We hope this Tool Kit together with its predecessor, ***Boomer Volunteer Engagement: Collaborate Today, Thrive Tomorrow***, will help your organization to grow, survive, and thrive. We know the journey is worth taking. Be patient, stay focused on results, be kind to yourselves, breathe…. Change will come and it will be worth it.

ABOUT THE AUTHORS

Jill Friedman Fixler is a thought leader on building organizational capacity through re-inventing, re-engineering, and re-vitalizing volunteer engagement. As Founder and President of JFFixler Group, Jill combines her skills as a consultant, trainer, facilitator, public speaker, and coach to share new volunteer engagement strategies with organizations throughout North America. Jill has more than thirty years of experience. Her nonprofit clients include health, human services, religious, government, cultural, environmental, and animal welfare organizations. She is co-author of *Boomer Volunteer Engagement, Collaborate Today, Thrive Tomorrow* (with Sandie Eichberg and Gail Lorenz, CVA) and has published numerous articles on volunteer engagement strategies and Board and organizational development. Jill currently co-authors the "Innovative Volunteer Strategies" eNewsletter and the "InnoVate" Blog at www.JFFixler.com and regularly speaks at national conferences in the United States and Canada.

Beth Steinhorn is a Senior Strategist with JFFixler Group and led the partnership with Metro Volunteers upon which this Tool Kit was based. Beth has more than two decades of experience in nonprofit organizations, including museums, education agencies, and faith-based organizations. She has served as an executive director, marketing director, educator, and evaluator. As a JFFixler Group Senior Strategist, Beth has consulted with museums, faith-based institutions, health organizations, and social service agencies. She leads the research efforts of the firm. She was the editor and project manager of *Boomer Volunteer Engagement, Collaborate Today, Thrive Tomorrow* and co-authors the "Innovative Volunteer Strategies" eNewsletter and the "InnoVate" Blog at www.JFFixler.com.